Refreshing. Restoring. Reorienting. I love the way Joel Clarkson
talks about God and life—reality—in his debut, *Sensing God*. He
speaks a timeless language—my language, our language—and is
in conversation with the great cloud of witnesses in the church
now and throughout the ages. Clarkson accentuates the good,
true, and beautiful in the reality of our lives and in creation,
beckoning us to stop, look, listen, taste, touch, and hear for
ourselves—to experience our triune God and the Kingdom with
our whole being. The book itself is a feast because it is steeped
in God's life. It is true and elicits joy. Through it, I have beheld
God. It is a book for such a time as this, and I couldn't be
gladder for it. I highly recommend it and look forward to more
from Clarkson!

> **MARLENA GRAVES,** author of *The Way Up Is Down*

I read this book on a summer day on the shore of Idaho's Priest
Lake, surrounded by timbered mountains. The effect it had on
me was a priestly one: mediating grace by fine-tuning my senses
to behold beauty and goodness, accompanied by the potent
reminder that one cannot grow in spirituality apart from growing
in sensuality. By the time I was done, I found that I had been
drawn into deeper intimacy with God through attentiveness to
and enjoyment of creation.

This is a book to take and read. Then taste and see—and
while you're at it, listen, smell, and touch—and know that God
is good.

> **ERIC E. PETERSON,** author of *Letters to a Young Pastor* and *Letters to a
> Young Congregation*

Both creation and the Incarnation show that God cares deeply about the stuff of earth. The problem is that most of us neglect capturing wonder in favor of productivity, efficiency, and hurry. Helping his readers develop a robust vocabulary of Christian imagination, Joel Clarkson gives us a feast for our senses. Theologically rooted, artistically curious, and reflective, *Sensing God* can help us learn again how to taste and see that the Lord is good.

ASHLEY HALES, author of *Finding Holy in the Suburbs* and *A Spacious Life*

God is at work within His world, but we do not always know how to recognize Him. Joel Clarkson, an artist and a theologian, guides us along the way of becoming fully alive to God. Exegeting poetry and nature, film and music, Scripture and the memories of his own life, he brings us to the edge of wonder and worship.

REV. DR. GLENN PACKIAM, associate senior pastor at New Life Church; author of *Blessed Broken Given*

In *Sensing God*, Joel Clarkson has given us a book which is both highly inspiring and remarkably down-to-earth. In Christ, the Word was made flesh, but too often, we disembody God and turn Him back into abstract theology. The reflections in this book will help us to find God where He chose to be found, right in the midst of life.

MALCOLM GUITE, author of *Sounding the Seasons*

SENSING GOD

Experiencing the
Divine in Nature, Food,
Music & Beauty

JOEL CLARKSON

A NavPress resource published in alliance
with Tyndale House Publishers

NavPress is the publishing ministry of The Navigators, an international Christian organization and leader in personal spiritual development. NavPress is committed to helping people grow spiritually and enjoy lives of meaning and hope through personal and group resources that are biblically rooted, culturally relevant, and highly practical.

For more information, visit NavPress.com.

Sensing God: Experiencing the Divine in Nature, Food, Music, and Beauty

Copyright © 2021 by Joel Clarkson. All rights reserved.

A NavPress resource published in alliance with Tyndale House Publishers.

NAVPRESS and the NavPress logo are registered trademarks of NavPress, The Navigators, Colorado Springs, CO. *TYNDALE* is a registered trademark of Tyndale House Ministries. Absence of ® in connection with marks of NavPress or other parties does not indicate an absence of registration of those marks.

The Team:
Don Pape, Publisher; David Zimmerman, Acquisitions Editor; Elizabeth Schroll, Copy Editor; Eva Winters, Designer

Cover illustrations by Eva Winters. Copyright © Tyndale House Ministries. All rights reserved. Inspired by photograph of blue mosque copyright © Fotosearch/Getty Images. All rights reserved. Cover photograph of gold texture by Katie Harp on Unsplash. Cover photograph of night sky by Wil Stewart on Unsplash. Cover photograph of stars by Casey Horner on Unsplash.

Author photo by Joy Clarkson, copyright © 2019. All rights reserved.

Published in association with The Bindery Agency, www.TheBinderyAgency.com.

Unless otherwise indicated, all Scripture quotations are taken from the *Holy Bible*, New Living Translation, copyright © 1996, 2004, 2015 by Tyndale House Foundation. Used by permission of Tyndale House Publishers, Carol Stream, Illinois 60188. All rights reserved. Scripture quotations marked NASB are taken from the New American Standard Bible,® copyright © 1960, 1962, 1963, 1968, 1971, 1972, 1973, 1975, 1977, 1995 by The Lockman Foundation. Used by permission. Scripture quotations marked NIV are taken from the Holy Bible, *New International Version*,® *NIV*.® Copyright © 1973, 1978, 1984, 2011 by Biblica, Inc.® Used by permission. All rights reserved worldwide.

Some of the anecdotal illustrations in this book are true to life and are included with the permission of the persons involved. All other illustrations are composites of real situations, and any resemblance to people living or dead is purely coincidental.

For information about special discounts for bulk purchases, please contact Tyndale House Publishers at csresponse@tyndale.com, or call 1-800-323-9400.

ISBN 978-1-64158-208-7

Printed in the United States of America

27	26	25	24	23	22	21
7	6	5	4	3	2	

For Mom,
who first taught me the steps
of God's glorious dance

CONTENTS

FOREWORD

An artist is made for a feast.

I practice my art in the reality created by such hopes for a Feast of the Lamb (Revelation 19:9). Pulverized minerals such as azurite and malachite are layered over and over onto paper or canvas over gold. Such extravagance and attitude may be met with skepticism in the realm of contemporary art, the very waters I swim in, or even in the academia of art. "Isn't art about being serious and dark?" "Isn't art about being transgressive?" "I thought art was poking fun at society?"

In art schools in the world today, you are told to deconstruct yourself. A "critique" is when your assumptions are dismantled. I've heard of students who are told not to use the words *beauty* or *creativity* because they connote an imperialistic past. While Christian schools may not be as brutal, the idea of "finding your voice" and being trained to be a "successful artist" is far from what these programs can promise, and many Christian schools mimic the secular to try to prepare the students for the "real" art world.

Many people do not know about the contemporary art world; the word *art* may conjure up works of commercially successful artists such as Thomas Kinkade. In such a transactional realm, the question of Feast is reduced and, well, commoditized to a consumer mind-set. Mall art is like fast food; it's perhaps the only accessible art to purchase for most people, but you should not consume too much of it. Instead, we are made for a Feast.

As this book attests, all humans, not just artists, are made for a Feast. In fact, the whole creation groans for it (Romans 8:22). Only through the trust of our senses, by refining our somatic knowledge, can we discover our ultimate path toward the new, through the banquet prepared in front of our enemies (Psalm 23:5).

Exodus 31 tells us that God gave Bezalel and Oholiab, two craftsmen filled with the Spirit, the ability to construct and also to teach. Our assumptions about making are further tested when we teach, to lead others to journey into the new. Students, I find, are hungry for sensory knowledge. What lies beyond our vista? What is art for? If there is no hope of our senses coming alive in that journey beyond, then why teach? If, as Joel Clarkson puts it, there is in education an "invitation of aroma" present toward the Feast, then that is worth leading and teaching. Even if there is a slight possibility that such a reality exists, it's worth motivating students to reach for it. Art exists for such deeper inquiries; sometimes it even creates a longing for that deeper journey.

I paint in my self-sequestered Princeton studio, using

Nihonga (Japanese-style painting) materials but for a contemporary art audience. My audience is considered mostly "secular." Azurite and malachite minerals are pulverized and mixed with nikawa (animal hide glue) by hand and layered over and over on Japanese hand-lifted paper. Such somatic knowledge leads to the intuitive, and over thirty years of experience flows out in a single stroke. At such times I "sense God" facing the fractures of our times, of violence and losses. Such a prismatic vision dispels the dichotomy of secular versus sacred: As all things are in the provenance of the sacred (though we twist them to create idols instead of giving God the glory), art can be attuned to our senses, to point toward the Feast.

How do we create, preparing for the Feast? At such times of deeper wrestlings, I pause to consider the Feast to come, breathe in the aroma of the new. To make, to teach, to live is to love. In a world where many acts of violence are called sense-less, this book lights the path toward a senses-full experience, now a necessary condition toward healing our fractured culture.

Makoto Fujimura, artist

INTRODUCTION

*Getting Good Dirt Under the Fingernails
of Our Senses*

At the end of my twelfth year, my family moved from the heat and smog of suburban Texas to the quietude of a Colorado home pressed up against the very edge of the foothills of the Rocky Mountains. For the first time in their lives, my parents decided to have our new home built from scratch, and for months, we waited in the Texas heat for weekly news of our Colorado bungalow, as builders slowly brought it into being. No detail was passed over; from kitchen fixtures to floral wallpaper patterns, we discussed each choice as a family, excitedly passing along our given selections. When we finally pulled up the long dirt road on a sunny June morning and turned into the driveway, it was exactly as we had imagined it, from soaring pines and quaking aspens to the wraparound porch, accentuating the enormous vista windows angled toward the steep rise of Mount Herman ahead. Everything was perfect.

Everything, that is, except the lawn.

To call it a lawn would have been, perhaps, deceiving, for the large, open area in front of the house was little more than a patch of dirt, jarringly unattractive in contrast to the otherwise idyllic mountain cove surrounding it on all sides. It had been bulldozed flat and even, which was its only redeeming feature, and loitered listlessly in front of the house like an uninvited guest. Our previous home had sported a half-acre grassy yard with room to run and explore, and the new yard stuck out like a sore thumb in contrast. Through some miscommunication, the lawn had remained unfinished, the only incomplete aspect of our mountain haven. It would be several days until the sod arrived for planting—sod that would transform it from a construction site into a proper grassy field.

The strange cognitive dissonance of the unfinished yard acted like a resonating chamber to the overflow of new experiences I encountered in our first days there. Everything was different; far from the humid, verdant green of central Texas, this landscape was stark and arresting, rising up in steep walls and jutting out at strange angles. The chilled, arid air of the evenings stung my breath, my lungs having not quite adjusted to the mile-high altitude yet. Instead of thick oaks with leafy, emerald canopies and soft humus beneath, pencil-thin evergreens towered over a brittle sandstone forest floor covered in prickly pine needles. At night, stars pressed out toward us with bright attention, not obscured by the dim glow of city lights to which we were so accustomed. The whole of the experience was alluring, yet I found myself feeling held at a distance. I wanted to draw close, to embrace this new orienting of my world, yet, like my lungs, my bearings remained unadjusted, always wheezing harder than usual to keep up with the constant stream of in-breaking novelties.

I can still recall, only a few days after moving in, the lumbering truck as it huffed into our driveway, looking like an overgrown, movable hill. The grassy sod my father had ordered had been piled in stacks of tens, and it shuddered like an earthquake when the driver turned off the truck. Carefully, each pallet was removed from the truck bed and placed in even rows at the long end of the yard, patiently waiting for someone to come and direct it toward its final occupation.

"What are we going to do with it?" I asked my father. "Plant it, of course," he replied. And the next day, we did. Piece by piece, we carried strips of the lush Kentucky bluegrass and began weaving it into the dusty expanse, first turning the soil so that we reached the damp loam beneath and sprinkling in growth supplement, then carefully and methodically laying out each strip. We patterned them like bricks, as if building a horizontal wall against the earth, pressing them tight, one against another, so that the seams melded into each other in perfect, unbroken lines.

At first, I was slow and cumbersome at my work, carefully lifting one strip at a time and keeping it away from myself to avoid unwanted stains; but soon enough, one strip had become two, and then three, and not too long in, my brother and I challenged each other to a contest of who could carry the most of the bluegrass at once, much to the chagrin of my father. Our blue jeans quickly took on a greenish hue as we rolled around in the lush carpet of grass beginning to stretch dozens of feet into the barren space. Our fingernails quickly filled with the darkened grime of dirt, and our faces somehow received the smudge of muddy joyfulness that can only come from close contact with soil. We made ourselves close at hand to the earth, taking up old, hardened clay and smudging it into newly softened turf. We knew that in so doing, it would more readily nourish the planted grass placed on it; little did we know, however, that it was already beginning to nourish us, planting the essence of that Colorado ground in our hearts and inviting us into participation in it.

When the sun started to set, we laid the final piece of sod and beheld our work, marveling in satisfaction at the emerald sea of wavy green grass before heading inside to clean up for dinner. Even though we all washed up, for days, we still had traces of soil in our hair and dirt under our fingernails. In retrospect, it seems a fitting image for what had happened to us. By drawing close to the mountain landscape, coming into tangible contact with the earth, letting it become a part of our experience, something had irreversibly changed. No longer were we uncertain of our new home, held at a distance; instead, we were invited into participation. That one day of laying the grass of our front yard became the entryway to years of beloved encounters with a Colorado landscape that still is near to my heart today, a home I can call to mind in the closeness of its very natural elements even thousands of miles away on the other side of the ocean.

You see, what I needed was not to think meaningful thoughts about my new home, trying to come to some understanding about it from a distance; what I needed was to come into real contact with it, to allow my senses to become immersed in its essence, to tangibly receive close at hand what I could not at arm's length. I needed to have *my senses engaged* in the good work of encounter.

Sensing God's Presence

As Christians, we long for more meaning in the midst of our busy lives. We often feel like we are missing out on something but can't put our fingers on what it is. We go to church and try to achieve a sense of deeper spirituality, but as soon as we walk out the doors, that feeling leaves, and we're back to square one. We know what we think about God and what we ought to believe, but what we believe so rarely escapes into the real world and sets its rhythms in our lives. We are *hungry* for more, *thirsty* to drink of deeper waters, seeking to *touch* the face of the divine. We want to *see* God's presence at work in every corner our lives. Isn't it amazing how so many of the ways that we talk about our growth in faith are *sensory metaphors?*

You can see it easily in contemporary worship songs, which are filled with these adjectives: "*Hungry*, I come to you / For I know You *satisfy.*" Or what about "I am desperate for a *touch* of heaven"? Or there's always the classic, "Open the *eyes* of my heart, Lord . . . / I want to *see* you."[1] Why is it that we use these sensory phrases for worship? There's no doubt that they are inspiring and expressive; could it also be that these images are powerful because our senses so shape our experience and outlook on life that we cannot escape their influence on us, even when we are raising our worship to the living God? Even more to the point, what if that is because God Himself has given us our senses to know Him on a deeper and more profound level?

I'm reminded of a moment in my early college years, when I was home on a brief break, sitting on the front porch with my mother after dinner. I had been sharing my doubts with her, the growing feeling of uncertainty and confusion in the midst of the intensity and constant change of my university life. I remember sharing with her how I had attended a service of worship during the week prior and left feeling utterly empty and uninspired. "I just don't feel the presence of God, Mom. It's like He's far away from me." She looked at me, surprised, and then laughed. "That's funny, because earlier tonight, we lit the candles for dinner and put on some of your favorite music. And then I served you a homemade meal, which I'm certain you told me was quite delicious and satisfying. And now, you and I are here in the cool summer evening air, looking out at a stunning sunset over the pines. It's beautiful, isn't it?"

She patted my back gently, and together, we watched and marveled as brilliant sunlight faded behind silhouettes of pines into the deep indigo of an August evening.

I've never forgotten that moment, and I've kept its lessons close to my heart over many years. When I am tempted to feel despair or sadness, to question faith or face unanswerable questions about the universe, I stop, get up, go to the kitchen, and make myself a cup of tea or coffee. I have a bite of something nourishing to eat, and then I put on some of my favorite music. After I'm feeling better, I sometimes go out for a walk and let the cool air refresh me. Just like in my childhood, when I got down in the dirt and laid the sod row by row, I let myself enter into contact with the world itself, pressing myself nearer to it, and by doing this, I draw closer to the presence of God hidden in every corner.

In recent years, some researchers in microbiology have affirmed the value of exposing children to soil at a young age, how the interaction with germs in everyday dirt actually strengthens the immune system and even provides enzymes that make it easier for a child's body to resist allergies and chronic conditions like asthma. Though the inclination is, of course, to keep kids from getting grimy and grubby, the research pushes in the other direction: Invest in the mess, it says. It is actually more harmful, some experts say, to over-sanitize, to protect children from the very elements which provide the means for their immune systems to naturally strengthen and grow. Healthy kids, suggests this line of thinking, are the ones who are getting dirt under their fingernails.[2]

What if our faith lives need the same thing? What if the answer we are looking for is not only to believe more fervently, to pray with more gusto, or have more holy thoughts, but to let those desires be heightened by getting the good earthen clay of God's holy world under the fingernails of our senses? What if, instead of simply trying to "be spiritual," we allowed our spiritual world to be informed by our sensory encounters in the world around us? Perhaps you have felt that no matter what you do, no matter how hard you work the muscles of your faith, somehow they just won't grow. Perhaps you feel they are even atrophying, losing the little bulk they already had, becoming weaker and weaker by the day. You feel far from the Lord, and you don't know how to find your way back. Can I suggest that perhaps the answer is not to try harder but to try something different? What if what you are seeking is hidden in plain sight all around you?

This is the journey of this book: to discover how Jesus is seeking us in the points of sensory contact embedded in every part of our lives. Jesus is calling us to get our hands messy with the work of faith rooted in the soil of the visible, the tangible, and the touchable—and to let that engaged work form and inform our witness to a world desperate for God's restoration. In this book, I invite you to walk with me into that exploration, to get dirt under your fingernails, not only to taste, but to touch, hear, smell, and see that the Lord is good; and that His goodness awaits us in countless sensory opportunities in the world every moment of our lives.

The Scope of Our Journey

Many of us have been taught to downplay experience, to think cautiously about how our senses might teach us. If there is another way, if our senses can, in fact, not only assist us in our spiritual lives but actually lead us into an encounter with Jesus Himself, then what is the precedent for that understanding of Christian practice? What is the shape of the theology which underpins that conviction? In the first two chapters of the book, we will explore the relationship between Jesus and His beautiful world, how He is the source and end of all beauty, and how our hearts sacramentally help us give meaning to what we encounter through our senses and return that encounter in praise to God.

In the remainder of the book, we will explore the whole of the sensory world, contemplating it through examples that engage with each of our senses and how they might help us to encounter God. In each of these chapters, I enter into the senses through manifested examples. I mention numerous poems and poets, theologians, writers, musicians, songs, excerpts from novels, experiences with food and drink, favorite places, and much more. I do so because the senses are encountered through *experience*, and my desire is that these examples help enliven your senses as you read about them. I want this book to be a resource for you, to fill you with new concepts and invite you into participation through your senses in the world itself. The examples I give are unapologetically drawn from the sensory things which have delighted, inspired, and convicted me, and I hope that you will see in them a possible parallel to the things that delight, inspire, and convict you.

In addition (and perhaps more importantly), I start each chapter with a story from my life. I do this because I believe, as you will discover more closely in the chapter on the sense of touch, we are more able to practice our sensory rhythms in close conversation with each other. We make an understanding of the world available through our shared community and communion that is not possible purely on our own. I hope you can see how true this is for me in the way that I turn to authors, artists, thinkers, leaders, friends, and family members over the course of this book to explain my own journey of sensing God. And I encourage you to identify people who may not be listed in this book—from friends and family members to admired public figures to artists and thinkers of all sorts—who may do the same for you. The most profound spiritual engagement through our senses is done in communion with the great cloud of witnesses who encourage us onward in our journey.

Ultimately, I write this book in the hopes that it will awaken your imagination for what it might mean to orient your senses toward the holy. My prayer is that you will become more aware of the scope of the senses in Christian experience, particularly in your own life; that you will feel equipped to understand more of how each sense opens an engagement with Jesus; and that you will feel exhorted to put your senses into practice, both for the sake of your own faith and for the sake of others.

Things This Book Is *Not*

One of the oldest practices in theology, going back to the early days of the church, is the expression of what is called *apophatic theology*. The term comes from a Greek word meaning "to deny," and the practice is in contrast to *cataphatic theology*, which comes from a word meaning, as you may expect, "to affirm."[3] Many of the church fathers found that while there are things we can say about God and the underpinnings of reality in a positive way, the world does not always fit into easy categories, and sometimes the best way to understand something is not to declare what it is but rather what it is *not*. Augustine, Gregory of Nyssa, and many of the fathers employed this *via negativa* (negative way) in their theology, and it has remained a powerful rhetorical tool used within and outside of Christian practice.

It is in the spirit of the *via negativa* that I want to articulate the scope of this book. Because the senses are by nature built around impression, experience, and affect, they are difficult to pin down with strong, declarative statements. With that knowledge in mind, here is my apophatic guide to what this book is *not*:

This book is not a *step-by-step, how-to guide* for using our five senses. As I explained above, my desire is to walk with you as a friend and an advocate, to guide you through a passageway in which you encounter various points of contact with sensory interaction. My intention is not to instruct your mind in *what to think* but rather to enliven your imagination for *how to engage*. This is not a book primarily concerned with telling you right or wrong ways of putting your senses to work but rather with making you aware of the multitude of different ways that God might meet us through our sensory perception. I sincerely hope that in reading this book, you won't walk away feeling that you have received some set of correct or exclusive rules for practicing your spirituality through your senses, but rather that you have received a foundation of ideas on which you can build through your own discernment—and through the work of the Holy Spirit in your life.

Because this book is not a user's manual for the senses, it is also not meant to act as *a comprehensive account* of how the senses are applied in the life of a Christian. In fact, very much in the spirit of awakening imagination, in each of the chapters on the rhythms of the senses, I intentionally focus on no more than one or two aspects of a given sense so as to give you *case studies which exemplify one among many ways of applying that sense*. For instance, in the chapter on hearing, I home in on music and don't discuss the spoken word. This is not because I don't value the spoken word or feel that there isn't much to be said about it but rather because I am myself a musician, and that vocation allows me a particular insight into the way music, as one subset of the sense of hearing, might open up our participation in Christ's work in the world. In another chapter, the chapter on touch, I focus on human contact, because this book is about encountering *Jesus* through our senses, and I wanted to focus on the way that Jesus Himself used touch as a way to heal and bring life to people around Him. However, there is a whole world of touch beyond human contact, and I hope some of the ideas in the chapter will perhaps prompt you to think of other ways that touch might lead us to participate in God's glorious world. Sometimes a chapter will even have overlapping senses, or a brief allusion to a sense which is covered in full in a different chapter; perhaps in this, you might come to realize how readily the senses interact with each other, and how rarely we use only one sensory faculty at a time, but rather combine multiple aspects to engage with the world in a multifaceted way. Everything that I bring to bear in this book I offer only as a jumping-off point, a resource to empower your imagination to apply these ideas beyond what I say here. Remember, my desire is not to give you the answers but to help you gain the tools to imagine, to ponder, and to engage.

This book is not meant to be an *exclusive doctrinal statement* about the senses, nor is it meant to be read as a theological treatise. I hope this book speaks to you in the space that you already inhabit, to encourage you to put into practice sensory rhythms right where you are. Like you, I come from a particular theological space, and I most certainly bring what I have learned in that space to bear in this book. However, I mention thinkers, writers, and artists both within and outside my tradition, including people from various backgrounds—Orthodox, Catholic, Evangelical, Calvinist, and beyond. Each of these thinkers has a unique viewpoint to offer, and each has influenced the way I think about my own faith. I am better for the breadth of their influence. I hope that in the same way, as you read this book, no matter your tradition, you will find meaningful ideas that resonate with your theological practice and help it to grow.

Finally, this book is not meant to provide a definitive answer of how we experience the divine through our senses. *Now, just wait a second,* you say. *What kind of trickery is this? Isn't that phrase in the very subtitle of this book?* Am I playing games, trying to sell you a bill of goods? Let me try to explain: This book is full of concepts that get at the idea of what a theology of the senses might be about. But I want you, dear reader, to hear me when I say that this book is only a starting point. And it *must* be that; for if the senses are to be our guide in encountering Jesus in a unique way, then you must take what you learn in these pages and put it into practice through your *experience*. The senses are their own sort of communication about God's presence in the world, a communication that is different than what can be related through words and ideas; they communicate through *encounter*. We use our minds to grasp complicated theories and tenets of faith, but if our senses in some way lead us to a knowledge of, or encounter with, the living God, then no words I can say here can express what can only be had through the knowledge which your sensory experience tells you. I can give you a perfect theoretical model for a theology of the senses, but unless you activate your senses and engage them in the trenches of the tangible world around you, seeking to find and respond to the presence of Christ there, this book will be for naught. I hope the fleeting taste you receive in this book will only serve to leave you hungry for much more and send you out into the world to dine at the rich table of the feast God has laid before our senses.

The wonderful thing is, your senses are already engaged with God's world in a million ways every day. From the people with whom you interact to the nature around you, from the meals you eat to the music which you listen to, it is my hope that this book will give you the *clarity to identify* the points of contact with the sensory world that shape your life on a day-to-day basis; the *insight to discern* how each of those areas might open up an interaction with the creator of the world who is speaking through His creation; and most importantly, the *courage to engage* with those points of contact and behold the glory of God through them.

Now that you know the scope of the journey, I invite you to join me. Let's go get some dirt under our fingernails.

1

LET BEAUTY AWAKEN

The Glory of God in the Stuff of the World

〜

The earth is full of thresholds where beauty
awaits the wonder of our gaze.

JOHN O'DONOHUE

I was able to taste the heat before I felt it. There had been a
hint of it in the air even with the air-conditioning blasting,
and when my father turned off the car, it took mere seconds
for the sweltering warmth to ooze into our car. It was a sticky
taste, full of dirt and cedar and pond water; and soon, it was
to become as familiar as a breath.

My family had moved to the middle of nowhere. Well,
actually, the middle of Texas. Locals would say that if you
took a pin and stuck it right in the middle of a map of Texas,
you'd hit Walnut Springs. Right there in the no-man's-
land between the soft, verdant landscape of East Texas and
the striking desert spread of West Texas, Bosque County

stubbornly held the gap as the unnoticed, ungainly sister between the two. And it was to this perceived limbo that my family moved, to live near my grandmother.

Of course, as a seven-year-old, I wasn't old enough to discern one sort of landscape from another, or put a value judgement on heat so palpable you could chew it up and swallow it. For me, everything was delightfully new: a sprawling ranch house, with an attic sufficiently large to allow my child-sized imagination room to romp around, instead of our previous house, a colonial structure that looked like every other two-story box on the street. The land behind that rancher, a veritable country in itself, was contained only by the barbed-wire boundaries at the edges of the two-hundred acres that comprised my grandmother's property.

There wasn't one part of those two hundred acres that I didn't love with my whole heart. My siblings and I would romp around the "tank"—a man-made fishing pond—with raucous glee, never managing to stay dry for any extended period of time. On other occasions, we'd amble down the dirt road stretching from our home to the back of the property, skirting around the deep ruts carved out by tires and fossilized into hardened molds by the elements. Once there, we'd veer from the road, taking a stealthy excursion through the tall Texas grass, always wary of snakes and other hidden critters. Finally, we'd go down the small, red dirt path, across the stream, and up the slippery embankment, where we'd arrive at our cabin.

The cabin rested on top of a small ledge, about five feet

above the water, though to my child eyes, it appeared to be dozens of feet in a vertical climb. It was a strangely arresting affair: The tiny box structure was composed of beams of crackly cedar all put one over the other, materials which we children had salvaged from a timber pile meant for fenceposts. The roof was a makeshift project consisting of a variety of dried grasses, which in the summer, always preserved enough pollen to reduce me to sneezing fits. There was no insulation, with gaping holes like lopsided prison bars appearing from the inside. But our cabin was hardly a prison; to us, it was a fortress, a place of security, joy, and happiness. Here we would make our homestead, our establishment. It was a small feat to the untrained eye, but to the expert eyes of a child, it was a masterpiece of architecture.

In those two summers before we moved back to the city, we explored and conquered every field, tree, and body of water and claimed it in the name of childhood. Our feet plunged through water and into squelching mud; our hands took hold of limestone and cedar, climbing and crawling our way through the adventures of undiscovered landscape; the heat of midday would distill into beads on our forehead, and just when it felt unbearable, a warm wind from nowhere would whisk across our faces in astonishing refreshment. When we grew weary of such toilsome exercises, we would retire to our fortress in the woods, where we would engage in a world of imagination, wild and set apart from the safe places of the world.

If you could have listened, you would have heard every field crying out in joy and all the trees clapping their hands in wonder and amazement at our childhood feats. I think the grass itself just might have bowed down in awe of the innocence and pure child delight that we exuded. Every shout for joy, every relishing of a rock or stream or tree was an unconscious act of praise on my part. My heart rose in thanksgiving for the beauty I beheld in each corner of creation in our little patch of Texas soil, and even if I wasn't yet able to speak the name hidden within every encounter of that glory, I knew, in my innermost parts, that it was true.

The beauty of nature has always held me firmly in its grasp. When I feel distant from the world, lost, and alone, I often plunge myself back into the midst of creation and listen for the voice on the wind that called to me as a child. I loved it with my whole heart when I was young, even though the singer of the song of nature was still hidden from me then. As I have grown older, the light of that glory has become cast in the shade of adult troubles, of financial challenges and family tragedies, of professional setbacks and private failures. The story of the gospel, of the death which sin brings and the life found in salvation, which felt so inconsequential as a child, has captured me. I find myself wrapped up in that narrative in a way I can't escape, in a way that has shaped me and drawn me to seek the light that redemption brings. The propositional truth of Christianity has become my story, an ordering of the world which rings as true as a church bell.

And yet, there is a part of me that knows I can only believe these things to be true because I have experienced the goodness of them all my life through the means of beauty. The song of nature has never left me void, and while pain and the experience of a broken world has compelled me to learn the name of the one who saves, I had already met Him long ago, in my childhood, and I still encounter Him day by day in the song of nature. When I was a child, my praise was an unspoken rising of the heart for the song sung by a hidden singer; now the singer has a name: Jesus.

The Singer of the Song of Creation

Jesus is the source of all beauty. In Him, creation had its beginning, and by turns, we, as His creation, were made to bear His image to the world. Just like all of creation, we, as created beings of God, are a physical manifestation of His love. This is a reflection of God's very nature, mirroring the Trinity itself: an eternal heavenly Father who, through the creativity of the Son and by the breath of the Spirit, transfigured a divine idea into the fullness of creation, a creation which finds its purpose and continuation in the incarnate Christ. John's Gospel begins with this in cosmic terms, echoing the beginning of the creation sequence in Genesis, in what some argue is the form of a hymn:

> In the beginning the Word already existed.
>> The Word was with God,
>> and the Word was God.
> He existed in the beginning with God.

God created everything through him,
and nothing was created except through him.
The Word gave life to everything that was created,
and his life brought light to everyone.[1]

Look at the way the text guides us from the eternal, universal reality of God down to the particularity of our time and space: First is the eternal Word, Christ, affirmed in His divinity; through Christ comes the magnificence of the created universe; and then, within that cosmos, humans are brought to life, participating in the one who illuminates that cosmos.

And when we were lost in our sin, Jesus, the Word who made the world, came into that world and became *part of it*. The work of salvation is on this cosmic scale because Jesus saved us, not by rescuing us *from the world*, but by *becoming part of it*. Jesus, as John so boldly puts it, is the *Logos*, the *Word*—an abstract thought, a concept—made *flesh*—tangible, existing in space and time, touchable, knowable. Before His crucifixion, death, resurrection, and ascension, before His miraculous earthly ministry, before His remarkable childhood and the dazzling events surrounding His birth—before any element of Jesus' life on earth, the first sign of God's salvation in Jesus is His incarnation, His taking on our flesh, the atoms and molecules of our existence, brought to life in the womb of His earthly mother. Jesus came into the midst of our time and space, stepping out of eternity into the very creation within which He brought us into being, and that in itself is a profound sign of redemptive love.

The apostle Paul echoes this extravagant connection between Christ and His masterful creation in the first chapter of Colossians, another passage also thought to perhaps be a hymn:

> Christ is the visible image of the invisible God.
> He existed before anything was created and is supreme
> > over all creation . . .
> Everything was created through him and for him.
> He existed before anything else,
> > and he holds all creation together.[2]

Paul doesn't let us escape his intended point, affirming twice that Jesus, as the origin of created existence, brings forth creation from His own essence, and that it continues to be sustained because of His presence within it. Creation is Jesus' own word, made into the flesh of the natural world. From microbes to galaxies, every corner of creation bears the imprint of its master artist. And just as John shows us, this activity isn't limited to that first act of creative expression through which we and the whole world came into being but is continued in God's redemption of the whole of creation in Jesus:

> through him God reconciled
> > everything to himself.
> He made peace with everything in heaven and on earth
> > by means of Christ's blood on the cross.[3]

Through Jesus, not only has God saved us from the consequences of our sin; in Jesus, the dying heart of a broken universe is being reversed. Creation is beautiful because it points to the beautiful one; the Father loves what His Son has created, and through His Son, He is making peace with "*everything* in heaven *and on earth*." What Jesus accomplished on the cross was more than a simple saving of souls. It was a reaffirmation all over again, hearkening back to that very moment of the creation of the universe, that what God has created is *very good* and is worth redeeming.

Christian storytellers have often been captivated by this relationship between God, creation, and redemption. One of the great Christian writers of the twentieth century, J. R. R. Tolkien, produced an imaginative interpretation of creation in his fantasy volume *The Silmarillion*. He imagined the world as a song sung by God, a metaphor which, as we will learn in chapter four, is as old as Christian faith itself.

In the opening pages of his epic history of his mythical world Middle Earth, Tolkien describes the creation of the universe by Illúvatar, who brought everything into being through a grand and glorious musical symphony. To his angelic servants, the Ainur, he gave the power to participate in that musical masterpiece by co-creating in harmony with Illúvatar's song. But one of the servants of Illúvatar, Melkor, was jealous of Illúvatar and attempted to make his own music, which quickly came into discord with Illúvatar's song, bringing strife into the good, true, and beautiful theme. Melkor seeks to drown out the beautiful theme of Illúvatar's creation.

To this violence and cacophony, Illúvatar responds to Melkor:

> And thou, Melkor, shalt see that no theme may be played that hath not its uttermost source in me . . . For he that attempteth this shall prove but mine instrument in the devising of things more wonderful, which he himself hath not imagined.[4]

Illúvatar makes clear that not only can the musical theme of creation which he has brought into being not be drowned out or destroyed, but even that which was intended for evil he will weave back into his theme for good.

The world God has created is not incidental to our redemption; it is precisely through the world He has created that He redeems it, by becoming part of it and consecrating it once again through His Son. In Jesus, we see the world with new eyes, for the God beyond our imagination has entered our universe. He has reclaimed the song of creation and woven it back into Himself.

If this is true, then the gospel becomes more than simply knowing the truth about Jesus intellectually, or even developing a relationship with Him spiritually. Though both of those things are truly good and necessary for a healthy walk with God, this understanding of the incarnation carries one more implication: that we behold Jesus' beauty *in His created world*, and that we become co-conspirators in the great work of manifesting that beauty in our day-to-day lives. We must learn to listen to Jesus' song in His world and become singers of it in turn. If the beauty within creation points us to the beautiful one, then when we fail to behold and respond to that beauty, we hide ourselves from Him.

Christ is the answer to the desires which emerge from our deepest parts. We long for beauty because we long for the one who is the source of beauty and who calls us back to life through the means of beauty in our lives. When we sin, it is often not that desire itself is wrong, but rather, that it is not aimed toward the only thing that can satisfy. Think of the seven deadly sins, alluded to in various parts of Scripture and brought into a more formal structure by the church fathers, sins in which, as the writer of Hebrews says, we become "so easily entangle[d]" (12:1, NIV). Lust emerges from the disorientation of the godly desire to consummate love, born from a self-giving which has been twisted into self-adulation. Pride is the disorientation of the rightful desire to belong, born out of a loss of the inward knowledge that we are God's children, sealed in His love. Wrath is a disorientation of the desire to be safe, born from a loss of the inward assurance of God's providence. Every sort of sin is desire for that which satisfies, that which delights, that which is beautiful, but cast away from its proper end in Jesus.

When we encounter sin in ourselves or others, our job is not to destroy the desire that was twisted and broken or downplay the potential longing for beauty within that misplaced affection, but rather to restore each to its proper alignment in Christ. How do we do this? By beholding the beauty of God's life in the world breaking through broken places, and by letting it shine out again in turn. It is precisely through those broken, imperfect longings that Jesus works His most spectacular feats of redemption, not by destroying them but by restoring them. The great songwriter Leonard Cohen powerfully grasps this work of grace in his song "Anthem": "Ring the bell that still can ring / Forget your perfect offering / There is a crack, a crack in everything / That's how the light gets in."[5]

Beauty, reoriented to the good and true God, revitalizes, softens, and restores, taking our broken desires and drawing them back into union with Him. When our hearts were stone, Jesus gave us hearts of flesh, because incarnation is always at the center of His work of salvation. First in Him, as the "firstfruits" of salvation, as 1 Corinthians 15:23 (NIV) tells us; and now, in us through Him.

Copying the Master Painter

In the Italian Renaissance, apprenticeship programs would place young men in the context of a master artist, a craftsman of the highest skill, who would relate his knowledge to his apprentice. The apprentice would live with the painter, first gaining a basic knowledge of materials, styles, and methods of application, and then later gaining an intimate understanding of the master's ways: his brush strokes, the way he contrasted light with shadow, the methods he used for proportion and substance. They would learn how to transform their artwork from something that would merely intrigue to something which might transform, something which would draw an observer in and change their understanding of the world. While the apprentice would likely eventually graduate onward up the artistic hierarchy of the time, they would always carry with them the gift of their master's style and technique. If they gained success and acclaim, it would be in large part because they had learned to apply their master's technique in their own, unique way.

We are apprentices of a master artist as well. When we set out to create, we do so in His style, by copying His technique. What are the hallmarks of the technique of our master artist?

We see them embedded in the world around us. Nature is our first sign of it: ordered symmetry and proportional harmony, in everything from pine cones to galaxies; sympathetic harmonic overtones, which align into exquisite harmonies; landscapes of breathtaking grandeur, which draw us into an engagement with the transcendent; vast distances between stars and planets, which express to us the limitlessness of the one who places those stars in the sky; light, which filters gently through leaves in summer or reflects off of waves breaking on the shore, which shines in the darkness and which the darkness cannot comprehend.

And that grand ocean of glory in the wide universe trickles down into everything that we experience day to day: the delight and glory of a beautiful melody; the enchantment of light as it shimmers through stained glass; the restorative kindness of a gentle embrace; the sudden, arresting joy of a fragrant aroma; the nourishing warmth of a good meal. Whether on a cosmic scale or in the mundane moments of our everyday existence, this divine expressivity presses out in every corner of our lives. As the coming chapters will reveal, every sensory encounter provides us a different way to engage with this artistry: Our interaction with music, whether listening or singing or composing, might become a way to emulate the symphonic mastery of a universe which harmonically unifies great diversity with great unity; visual art might allow us to express the way in which the world presses out with the illumination of the divine and becomes a means through which we are seen and consecrated by the God who has turned His face toward us; the sense of touch, and the capacity to give it as a gift to others, might recall to mind how God entered this world as one of us and gave His life as a gift of healing for all; and taste and aroma bring us into the awareness of the abundance with which the world overflows, a plenitude which blesses and nourishes our lives, in the same way that God's overflowing goodness is given to us as a free gift of grace.

In these ways, we are able to imitate the creative work of our master and more readily reveal His love and grace to the world around us. The more we behold Jesus' beauty in His own creation, and the more we bear witness to that beauty through our own emulation of our master artist, the more we bring the glorious light of the gospel into brighter clarity.

When We Miss the Glory

The two ideas we've discussed so far—that we are meant to behold Jesus' beauty in the world as a sign of His redemptive work and are then meant to reveal that beauty to others—aren't only valuable; they are invaluable. Seeing Christ for who He is and bearing witness to His loveliness is imperative for knowing Him and learning to love Him. The apostle Peter learned this the hard way.[6]

He had already been rebuked once. Mere days before going up on the mountain with Jesus, James, and John, he had told his Lord he would never allow the authorities to take Jesus and harm Him. Jesus had reprimanded him as "Satan," a statement that planted a fear deep in his heart. He was afraid of what might happen to the Master, and even more afraid of what the Master might *allow* to happen.

Thus, when he saw Jesus shining out in glorious, blinding light on the mountain, and the fear rose up within him again, his intention to understand, to make sense of what was before him, kicked right back in. Here was a moment of divine revelation, with the very heroes of the Jewish people, Moses and Elijah, joining them there. Peter's mind raced; perhaps they needed to build tabernacles for Moses and Elijah, usher this profound vision into the midst of the people. Maybe Jesus wouldn't have to suffer after all. Maybe there was a way to triumph *and* prove their enemies wrong. Perhaps this is what the vision meant; if he could define it, understand it, perhaps then the fear would melt away once more.

He had only just started to speak when a thunderous voice from above decimated any remaining words within him, rendering him as silent and still as the grave. *This is my Son, whom I love. Listen to Him!* Peter knelt, humiliated and terrified, not knowing what to think or say. He knew now that everything he had imagined about Jesus was too small, inconsequential. Perhaps for the first time, the reality of this man's true identity began to seep into him, the bright whiteness searing the edges of his consciousness. The voice had commanded him to listen to Jesus, and now, Jesus' troubling words came back to him in a rush. What Jesus had predicted of His own death frightened Peter deeply, but in a way, this new understanding of Jesus, as the glorified one, waiting to be raised up, put an even deeper fear in Peter. The vision of Jesus there between the two great prophets of old was beautiful beyond imagination, and Peter couldn't control it; he understood that now. He was meant to behold it, but he wasn't ready to behold such glory; it required nothing less than his transformation, a transformation not yet complete within him. And yet, as Peter crouched, hunched over and trembling, Jesus placed His hand on Peter's shoulder, bringing him back to his feet. "Get up; don't be afraid." Filled with unknowing, but holding the hand of his master, Peter began to descend the mountain.

You see, we are much like Peter. Much of our faith is wrapped up in constructing "tabernacles," spaces in which we can come to certain conclusions, have a sense of understanding. We have apologetics to help undergird the reasonableness of Christian faith, and Bible-study tools to make sense of the Scripture we read. Often, the sermons we listen to are built around giving us a "takeaway," and when we discuss our growth in faith, we articulate it through what we have *learned*, the life lessons we have gained. In short, our faith often revolves around the things we can comprehend and integrate into our lives in an orderly way. Is there anything fundamentally wrong with this sort of tabernacle construction? Absolutely not; on the contrary, the gospel is fundamentally the good news of Jesus. That good news must be expressed, both to ourselves and to others. It must be said explicitly. Without that knowledge, we lack the ability to articulate the very foundations of our faith.

And yet, knowledge is incomplete without a change of our hearts; this is because the one in whom we find "the hope of glory" is not a *what*, but a *who*.[7] We are not made ultimately to understand God but to adore Him, to draw close to Him and participate in His glory through Jesus, as Romans 8:17 tells us. That sort of passion can't be contained in understanding alone; it must allow itself to be carried forward in experience of the infinite, eternal God who has made Himself close to us in Christ. And God has given us our five senses to engage in that experience. Not only are our senses not something to spurn or regard suspiciously; instead, they are a very real and manifest means through which we draw close to our Lord, experience His glory.

Moses and Elijah understood; in their own lives, they had each been given the privilege of witnessing the very presence of God up close. Moses was given a brief glance of God's "back," and the mere passing glimpse caused His face to shine in glory. Elijah was given the incredible privilege of participating in that glory, riding a chariot of fire into heaven itself. In the transfiguration, they stood as witnesses, testifying to the transforming power of simply beholding God's beauty.

Peter's failure was a failure to *behold beauty*. In his intent to create a narrative that made sense of the phenomenon before him, he failed to allow the glory before him to transform him. You see, when we behold Jesus' beauty through the sensory points of contact in the world around us, it begins to change our hearts. It plants that unspoken Word—that incorporeal idea from before time itself—in our very being, Christ incarnated in us. To behold God's glory in the world He has created is to allow Jesus to transfigure us by planting His glorious transfiguration light in our hearts.

And just as the transfiguration was the vision of what Jesus would become through His death and resurrection, so Jesus within us is also a sort of transfiguration, a vision to others of what each of us will one day be when heaven and earth are restored to perfect unity in Him. When we engage with Jesus' beauty in the world around us, and allow it to shape us, we bear the beauty of that transfigured light within us, shining like a beacon in a dark world. In so doing, we invite Christ's incarnational power to flow into us and exponentially onward into every corner of our world. Every part of our lives, from the luminous to the mundane—even our day-to-day tabernacle moments—might be transfigured, shining as a testament to the one whom each of those elements is meant to glorify: Jesus.

Thinning the Veil

This is because Jesus isn't only the source and the sustenance of beauty. He is also the *end* of beauty, the final point toward which all our desires as Christians are aligned. From our journey thus far, we know that through Jesus' incarnation, life, and death on the cross, eternity stepped into time, declaring God's creation worth redeeming. But in Jesus' resurrection and ascension, the places are swapped, and time is drawn into eternity. Jesus, the perfect man, more holistically human than we in our imperfect humanness can imagine, rose bodily into heaven, carrying His incarnated flesh into eternity, declaring that not only is creation *good*, it is *destined for redemption*. Our witness of beauty in the here and now is a foretaste of what is coming someday, and when we celebrate that beauty and give it back to our hurting world, we not only honor Jesus, but also create a touchpoint for the eternal, making it palpable in our present moment.

Every time we cherish a beautiful sunset or relish a cool wind on our face, whenever we bask in the glory of sunlight or delight in the restoring grace of rain—every instance in which we reckon with God's beautiful created world and our heart rises in praise—not only are we *beholding* Jesus' hidden presence, we are also *declaring* it to be a faithful promise of what is yet to come.

Though we are still in the broken place, waiting in sorrow behind the veil that sin has woven out of death, when we behold Jesus' beauty, the weave grows just a bit more threadbare. We create what the ancient Celts called "thin places," points where the divide between heaven and earth grows less defined, and we are able to catch a glimpse of our final hope. Each time we allow Christ's beauty to take hold in our lives, we become a living testimony toward what is often called the "Beatific Vision," the moment when that veil of death is torn in two forever, and we behold Christ face-to-face in His resurrection glory. If we learn to behold Christ's beauty in each part of our lives as Christians in the time and space within which God has placed us—right here, right now, moment by moment—every engagement of our senses toward experiencing Jesus' glory can be a promise toward the day we all long for, the day in which our desires and the fulfillment of those desires will no longer be separated, a time when we will behold Him, the beautiful one, face-to-face for all of eternity.

Even now, so far separated from my childhood days in the heat of a Texas summer, I still believe that the trees in the fields are clapping their hands, and the grass bows down in worship. I believe, with the psalmist, that "The heavens proclaim the glory of God,"[8] and that "their message has gone throughout the earth."[9] Often in my distraction, uncertainty, and confusion, I fail to recognize, forget to look up, miss the glory; and yet, when, by grace, my eyes are raised again, and I catch the strains of that cosmic harmony, I realize that the song of glory in the world has never ceased. And in that realization, I know in my heart that their praise is not simply a spectacle, something for me to observe; it is a challenge, an admonition: Will you join in the song? Will you, too, give praise to the one through whom all things came to be, and in whom all things will be put to rights again?

COMMON SENSES

- Look through the Psalms for five to ten statements that the psalmists make about creation. How do they describe creation? The relationship between God and nature? Do the psalmists portray God's presence in nature, and if so, how? How might the psalmists' words about creation change the way you think about creation?

- Take a walk near where you live. Identify at least three things that are beautiful or delightful—anything from flowers, to birdsong, to freshly mown grass, to the smell of tacos from your favorite taco shop! As you recognize each beautiful thing, let your heart say a small prayer of thanks.

2

TO RISE WITH THE MORNING STAR

*How the Heart Receives and Transforms
What Our Senses Tell Us*

⌒

Have your heart right with Christ, and he will
visit you often, and so turn weekdays into
Sundays, meals into sacraments, homes into
temples, and earth into heaven.

C. H. SPURGEON

The hour was early; far before the rising of the sun. The whole house was drenched in a heavy, slumbering silence. Only the methodical breath of my brother asleep on the other side of the room edged its way into the field of stillness in which I found myself. I lay awake, trying with all the strength of my eight-year-old mind not to feel fear at the persistent darkness, not yet relinquishing its grasp on the early morning hours.

In the kitchen at the bottom of the stairs leading up to our room—the "boys' room"—*I heard footsteps.* This would have added to my fear if not for the fact that I knew who was quietly passing by below. I slipped out of bed and walked down the stairs. Sure enough, my mother was there, dressed and on the cusp of escaping out of our sliding glass door and into the humid Texas air.

My mother has always cherished early morning hours. It is her time to gather the world to herself, fill the four corners of her spirit with the peace and joy of God. Throughout my life, whenever I have been home with my family, my morning liturgy has always included walking into the main living spaces of our home to find my mother with a cup of tea in one hand, a Bible in the other, a candle lit on a nearby table, and some sort of instrumental music playing in the background. Her rhythms of grace have always exuded a particular radiance in those hours near dawn, as if daring the sun, upon its arrival, to meet the vitality of her spirited love for her God and the life she has been given. Those moments of aloneness in the presence of silence are sacred for her and have been for as long as I can remember.

Perhaps they were even more so then, with four rambunctious children aged ten and under, ranging with limitless energy throughout her home from dawn until long after dusk. Perhaps the chance to pound pavement and feel the cool of morning air fill her lungs before the thickness of both the summer heat and joyful chaos of her family descended on her day was as sacred an act as sitting quietly reading Scripture. In any case, it came as no surprise to me to find my mother slipping out the door for a walk.

"Can I go with you?"

My own words sounded louder than I was expecting in the silence. My mother looked back from the door, regarding me for only a moment, and then gently shushed me with a finger to her mouth and pointed to my sneakers. I smiled excitedly. Two minutes later, I walked out behind her into the early morning air.

We trudged along in silence at first. While I was simply enjoying the world around me in my introverted, quiet way, I'm certain my mother was reorienting her expectations for the moment. Little could I have known at the time what a gift she was giving me by allowing me to share in what she intentionally set apart as her own moment of solitude. I held her hand and strained to feel the stagnant air broken by the wayward drift of a cool breeze. The dirt of the hilly road under our feet scrunched in a lopsided rhythm, my legs taking nearly two strides to each one of my mother's. In the distance, between the thick oaks that gathered on either side of the road, I could see a sliver of where the land ended and sky began. The horizon was pregnant with the impending dawn, a warm arc of crimson and amber bubbling up into the dark expanse above. I followed the gradient colors into the fading sky, where, directly in our line of sight, a single star still stubbornly held on to its spot in the heavens, refusing to surrender to the rising light. My child imagination was caught in a dazzled wonder, and without knowing it, my finger sought out the lonely star. "Look!"

My mother, cast in the throes of her own inner world, regarded me, and then the awaiting sight. She smiled and stopped for a moment. "It's beautiful, isn't it? Do you know what star that is?"

I shook my head, curiosity rising up within, knowing from my mother's words that this star was a *known* star, a star that meant something.

She looked back to the sky thoughtfully. "That's the morning star. You wouldn't know it from looking at it, but it's actually a planet, Venus. It's so bright because it's reflecting the light of the sun, and it will stay like that until right before the sun comes up."

We began walking again. The dawn was growing, on the edge of bursting out over the landscape like gold plating, and yet that stubborn orb above was holding on, burning its brightness with all its might, refusing to relinquish its place in the sky. I heard my mother's voice again.

"Did you know that Jesus is the morning star too? It says in the Bible that He'll rise in our hearts when the morning comes." I looked up at her, and she returned my gaze with a smile as she squeezed my hand. "Don't ever forget that. When Jesus comes into your heart, you can always know that He brings the light of goodness and beauty with Him."

We continued to trudge down the road in silence. No more than a few seconds later, as if on cue from a conductor, a sudden symphony of color exploded over the Texas landscape. Burnished bronze reflected off rippling leaves, and an abrupt rush of wind caused the thick grass on either side to shudder in a golden shimmer of shocked brilliance. Everything in sight, from pond water to the pebbles on the road, glowed, as if filled and animated with the potency of life.

I looked up; the morning star had disappeared, allowing

itself to be fused into the light of the real and present dawn all around us. Morning had come.

By inviting me to participate in her engagement with the beauty of creation, and by connecting that encounter with the person who is the source of that beauty—Christ—my mother planted a *sacramental* bond in my heart, a touchpoint with the presence of the divine. It was not that we created it through our actions; surely the hidden presence of Jesus was already at work in countless sunrises stretching back to the dawn of time. She simply opened my eyes to recognize it in my space and time and respond to it in worship.

More Than a Symbol

From the beginning of Christianity, believers have held that there are tangible signs that connect our lives to God's eternal reality through our participation in them, imbuing our day-to-day lives with a heavenly grace. The earliest signs appeared in Christian worship, and we still know and practice them today: Communion and Baptism. These signs weren't seen as merely symbolic, inanimate gestures, but rather were considered to be imbued with a heavenly grace being made present in the here and now, from the love of the Father's heavenly heart, through the incarnation of the Son's presence, and in the power of the Spirit. And they were constituted from manifest elements of the world itself; bread and wine in Communion, and water in Baptism. Saint Augustine described a sacrament as "an outward and visible sign of an inward and invisible grace." In other words, a sacrament embodies what is already happening in heavenly realms beyond our limited existence here on earth, providing a tangible expression of an eternal reality. A sacrament is a living engagement of the physical in the spiritual, of the time-bound in the eternal; and the sacraments of the church focalize in worship what is already true about the whole world: that the whole of the universe is itself sacramental, nature intertwined with the activity of Christ moving in and through it.

In fact, we are *not even able* to be mere observers of a reality which is so inextricably bound up in the person of Christ that it is through His authority that the universe continues to be sustained day to day, moment to moment, second to second. Hebrews 1 tells us that "The Son radiates God's own glory and expresses the very character of God, and he sustains everything by the mighty power of his command."[1] As elements of creation, we ourselves are sustained by Christ, down to the breath we breathe every moment. And yet, as beings made in the image of God, through the sacramental reality at hand—Jesus radiating God's glory through creation—we are given the capacity to recognize and participate in that glorious, persistent presence of Christ in His created world. It is a mystery which we can never fully understand empirically, yet through the redemptive work of the Holy Spirit within us, we are able to experience, gaining knowledge of the truth not through intellectual comprehension but rather through encounter.

Hans Boersma, professor of theology at Regent University, articulates it this way:

> It seems to me that the shape of the cosmic tapestry is one in which earthly signs and heavenly realities are intimately woven together, so much so that we cannot have the former without the latter.... The reason for the mysterious character of the world ... is that it participates in some greater reality, from which it derives its *being* and its *value*.[2]

In other words, both the created order and how each element is placed within it is designed specifically by Jesus, sustained through Him, and finds its completion in Him. We, like the rest of God's creation, were created with a unique purpose; and yet unlike every other being in creation, we are given eyes to see the ongoing phenomena at hand and to participate in it by choice, aligning the rhythm of our existence with the song creation sings instinctually in praise of its sustaining creator. And this miracle is accomplished through the crux of the sacramental within us: our hearts.

Heart Work

Depending on the translation of Scripture, the word *heart* is used in various forms over five hundred times. The heart plays as a center point, a catalyst, between what we observe of the world around us and conclude philosophically about it and what we then enact back into that same world through our actions and words. Proverbs says to "watch over your heart with all diligence, for from it flow the springs of life."[3] Jesus returns to this idea centuries later, boldly declaring to the religious leaders of the day, "It's not what goes into your mouth that defiles you; you are defiled by the words that come out of your mouth. . . . For from the heart come evil thoughts, murder, adultery, all sexual immorality, theft, lying, and slander. These are what defile you."[4] In short, that which we will into being through our passions is a sign of what we value. Our heart has great power to plant seeds of beauty or to sow havoc; out of our hearts, we speak of the truth we believe of the world. As Proverbs says, "As water reflects the face, so one's life reflects the heart."[5]

You see, we are built for more than mere information; we are made to take information and assign meaning to it. C. S. Lewis said that "reason is the natural organ of truth; but imagination is the organ of meaning. Imagination, producing new metaphors or revivifying old, is not the cause of truth, but its condition."[6] Our imagination, the engine of our hearts, will necessarily seek to assign meaning to the truth we receive. Without the heart, information would remain nothing more than a collection of facts. Facts have no interest in being revealed to the world because they have no inherent value; truth without meaning is static and inanimate. When the mind is paired with the heart, however, we are driven to find meaning in information; through our hearts, we assign meaning to that which we know, interpreting it according to our passions and desires. And out of the imagination of our hearts, we create sacramental manifestations of what we believe of the truth, through our words and our actions.

Our hearts are engines of sacrament.

The common wisdom of much of contemporary Christianity pushes fiercely against this notion. We are prone to downplay the power of desire—and of the heart to seek what it desires. It is more comfortable to think we can maintain our autonomy and approach God as if we are equal parties mutually agreeing to terms. When we hear the psalmist say to "Take delight in the LORD, and he will give you the desires of your heart,"[7] or when Proverbs tells us to "Trust in the LORD . . . and he will make your paths straight,"[8] we often hear a quid-pro-quo offering: I give you what you want, and you give me what I want. *You get my trust and delight, God, and I'll get what I desire and a clear path laid out for me.* We pray over these verses as a charm toward the things we want in our lives, thinking of ourselves in the driver's seat and God as the one who fills up the tank whenever we need it.

What if, instead of God simply giving us what we desire, this verse is suggesting an opposite sort of satisfaction? What if there is a grander reality at play in which God's eternal goodness is piercing through the fabric of our own time and space through His Son? What if, instead of getting what we want by doing what God asks, God is inviting us to let go of our own desires, our own rights, our own sense of the way the world works because He wants to transform our vision and help us truly see? When we align our hearts to God's heart, it's not that we get what we desire; it's that He recreates and redirects our desires toward that which truly satisfies. We let go of the simplistic things we once wanted because we are given something far more magnificent. We are given the opportunity to see the world as it is.

The inner eyes of our hearts are opened to the only true reality, so that our hearts may desire the only thing which truly satisfies. *Our very desires themselves are changed.*

In the words of Augustine, long a pursuer of worldly, perverse desires before finally relenting to the pursuit of the Holy Spirit, "you have so made us that we long for you, and our heart is restless until it rests in you."[9]

The world is sacramental, yes, because through Jesus, creation itself participates in the testimony of the great and beautiful and eternal God. But even more importantly, *we* are sacramental because we were made to recognize that testimony, to allow our hearts to be transformed by it, and in turn, to return our rightly aligned passions back into the world sacramentally through everything we do and say. God is constantly calling us into His heavenly reality, longing to give us eyes to see. All of creation is haunted by heaven, and when we are brought into Christ's story, we see that it is His presence pressing out through all things, calling the world back to reconciliation with God through His new life. Jesus has drawn the story of our time and space into God's eternal, heavenly story. And through us, God intends to make His heavenly reality present in the very moment of our place in history.

The Here and Now of the Coming Kingdom

God intends His eternal heavenly Kingdom to be mediated through the story which was begun in the Garden, continued through His intervention in the story of Israel, redeemed through Jesus, and consecrated in the hearts of all who allow Christ to enter their stories and transfigure them. The story into which we are being transfigured is the Kingdom of heaven, a new and living reality, in which the eternal perfection and goodness of heaven, which will one day be complete by becoming manifest on earth, is breaking through our time and space and already beginning the work of redemption.

Thus, each of us who have Christ within us are living in a constant paradox. On the one hand, we still exist in a broken world, a place where sin and death still seem to rule with impunity. If anything, things seem to be getting worse, not better. Social and familial brokenness is commonplace, and isolation is the new normal. Sectarianism and political polarization is on the rise, and it is harder and harder for people of varying worldviews to find ways to dialogue. The epidemic of war plagues many countries, laying waste to whole cultures, and ever-present, looming specters of apocalyptic occurrences, from pandemic illnesses to the abiding terror of nuclear warfare, never seem to stray far from headlines. Strife, sadness, and discord are ever at the fringes of our contemporary lives and sometimes even press unavoidably into the center of our focus.

Particularly in light of the horrors of the twentieth century, with its multiple world wars and untold death and desolation caused by the cruelty of totalitarian regimes and revolutions, modern Christianity has had to face this onslaught of darkness in an unprecedented way, and often, it has fallen captive to the dualism present in much of modern thought. When something tragic or wicked happens, which causes pain and suffering, our tendency is to wonder if good can win in the face of such evil. We compare the seeming quantity of evil to the good we quantify through our own vision and are often led into despair when evil persists.

This is not the way of Christ. In His Kingdom, the two are not forces grappling with each other for the upper hand. Evil, no matter how profound or widespread, is never an equal and opposite balance to good. Rather, the good of Christ's Kingdom is an eternal reality breaking into the broken world, and the days of the seeming ruler of our current time and space—*death*—are numbered. Death is dying, and Christ's Kingdom is coming to reign eternal. Through the Resurrection, we are given new eyes to see, eyes which are unafraid of death because the eternal mending power of resurrection is our destiny. By enduring death, first of our old spiritual selves and then of our current frail bodies, we remove from death its only power, rendering it powerless. An ancient Easter hymn expresses this with vivid language:

> Christ is risen from the dead, trampling down
>   death by death,
> and upon those in the tombs bestowing life![10]

Through Christ in us, we are trampling down death by means of death's only power over us. By entering the story of Christ's death and resurrection and participating in it, we are recognizing Christ's new Kingdom, which is coming to restore all things.

And yet, this is more than simple recognition. It would not be enough for us to endure the evil and suffering in our lives and in the lives of those around us with the mere promise of that which is to come. By partaking of the formal sacraments of the church, and through letting those sacraments reorient our vision of the world, we participate in the coming Kingdom by drawing the *someday* of it into the *here and now*. We are not simply pointing toward a reality which will eventually have victory over this reality; through sacrament, we are entering a new reality in this very moment in our history. And even more profoundly, this reality isn't something which transcends, alters, or disregards our world but something which shows what it was meant to be—and will be again someday. Alexander Schmemann gives voice to this in his excellent book, *For the Life of the World*:

> A sacrament . . . is always a *passage*, a *transformation*. Yet it is not a "passage" into "supernature," but into the Kingdom of God, the world to come, into the very reality of this world and its life as redeemed and restored by Christ. It . . . is not a "miracle" by which God breaks, so to speak, the "laws of nature," but the manifestation of the ultimate Truth about the world and life, man and nature, the Truth which is Christ.[11]

This new reality—the Kingdom of God—makes present to us the world as it is meant to be and will be again through the restoration of Christ in the fullness of time. We are heralds of that vision, and by participating in the life piercing through the darkness and sin of our world, we bring it into clarity for ourselves, our congregational communities, and for the whole world.

In S. D. Smith's adventurous children's fantasy story *The Green Ember*, rabbit siblings Picket and Heather have fled their home, separated from their parents and little brother, and find themselves refugees at Cloud Mountain, a protected community hidden away amid war and destruction. The Lords of Prey, hordes of ravenous wolves and sinister raptors, have razed the Great Wood, the home of rabbit-kind, by burning every inch in their reach, and rabbits from every corner of the Great Wood have taken up shelter at Cloud Mountain. Given the imminent threat of violence and terror all around, Heather and Picket are surprised to see that the people of Cloud Mountain persist in seemingly unwarlike activities: painting, sculpting, baking, trimming hedges. Heather asks Maggie "O'Sage," a wise elder of Cloud Mountain, why this is. Maggie explains:

> Here we anticipate the Mended Wood, the Great Wood healed. Those painters . . . are really seeing, but it's a different kind of sight. They anticipate the Mended Wood. So do all in this community in our various ways.
>
> We sing about it. We paint it. We make crutches and soups and have gardens and weddings and babies. This is

a place out of time. A window into the past and the future world. We are heralds, you see, my dear, saying what will surely come.[12]

In the economy of God's Kingdom, we are more than those who hope; we are those who anticipate what we are assured is coming by observing and responding to the world all around us. In sacrament, Christ, as the Living Word, brings the story of redemption to life within us, recreating the drama in our present time, and gives us vision to see *right now* what we believe by faith is to come. Rather than simply asking us to trust Him that it's true and put our hope in a future event, Christ's reality makes what's ahead of us real in our hearts in the here and now.

Stepping-Stones into the Kingdom

Just as Christ is the particular revelation within an inherently sacramental universe, the enactment of His story in and among His people has always been through particular sacramental signs, practiced in gathered Christian worship. These signs recall the story of Christ's dynamic Kingdom into our present and invite us to participate in that story. They are public and corporate, always drawing us out of our individual selves and into the shared narrative. They require us in our entirety, not only a portion of our expression but the remaking of our whole self, body and soul. Through them, we allow ourselves to be initiated and sustained by the story, toward the end that awaits all Christians: being formed into the image and likeness of Christ and drawn ever more deeply into His life.

Though various traditions practice a variety of formal sacraments, nearly all churches recognize two fundamental sacraments for the initiation into and continuation of life within the body of Christ: Baptism and the Eucharist. These two sacraments are crucial not only for how they shape us in worship but for how they reverberate beyond the bounds of our worship, their meaning spilling out into the world through what we do in our lives every day, and particularly through our engagement with the sensory aspects in that world. These two sacraments give narrative scope to the Christian journey: Baptism marks an entry into the story of Christ's Kingdom; and the Communion table—or as it is often referred to more traditionally, the Eucharist—marks the continuation of that story through the continual return to Christ's gift of Himself.

Through Baptism, we begin our journey into God's Kingdom, dying to the old vision of the world and being given new sight. We are given eyes and ears of the heart, to see the presence of Jesus entering into broken things and stoking the embers of new life, and to hear the song of recreation reharmonizing the lost parts of the world and weaving them into the symphony of the coming Kingdom. The spiritual life which has been given to us in Christ will be real in our bodies, too, someday. We are the heralds of that vision, and when we participate in Baptism, we are choosing to allow our hearts to be transformed, so that we see from the inside out.

This process involves our first true participation in the death and resurrection of Christ. The Episcopal Book of Common Prayer says that through the water of Baptism, we are "buried with Christ in his death," and that by it we "share in his resurrection."[13] As we are submerged, we allow our old spiritual selves to be buried, and along with it, all the sin, self-centeredness, and despair that ruled our former selves. We do this because we know that as we return upward through the waters of Baptism, our souls are brought back from the death of sin by allowing the death within us to die. And we are resurrected into a new and everlasting life, a life hidden with Christ in God. In the early church, those who were baptized were described as "illuminated," set afire with the light of Christ through the coming of the Holy Spirit.[14] In Baptism, the darkness and shadow of sin is allowed to die, so that through us, Christ's light might shine out as a witness to the reality of His heavenly life breaking into the world through us.

In this way, Baptism begins our journey, but it also hearkens forward to what our end will be in the fullness of our time on earth. Just as through water Baptism, we express the dying of our old selves so that Christ may enliven our souls and breathe life into us through the Holy Spirit, when we pass through physical death, we allow our old, world-worn, broken bodies to pass away, trusting in Jesus' resurrection power, that He is restoring the world He created, and that in so doing, He will restore us as part of it. Just as we signify the coming of new life into our spiritual selves in water Baptism, in death, we relinquish the hold on our sinful bodies, knowing we will receive God's new life in the body in Jesus' resurrection. In this way, Baptism provides the bookends to our story on earth, and when we participate in the sacrament of Baptism, we proclaim the coming Kingdom, a Kingdom in which creation itself will be redeemed and restored.

And yet, we are still attached to a broken world, and it is easy for our vision to grow dim. We need Jesus every moment, to sustain us, to remind us to whom we belong—and who is the true reigning King of the Kingdom already present in us. Through the sorrow and sin of the world, which even comes back to haunt us who have been illumined by the Spirit, our light grows dim. Into this need, Jesus gives Himself. The Eucharist is the highest and most profound moment of our participation in worship because it alludes to the most fundamental underlying truth of our Christian faith: that it is never by our own action that we approach God, but it is through Christ's gift of Himself that we are restored to the source of our life and sustained day by day. To receive the Communion elements is to abandon our temptation to resurrect the "old man" and instead accept Jesus' life as our whole sustenance, body and soul. It is to return our hearts to the most fundamental thing they were made for: praise of our creator.

The root Greek word from which Eucharist is derived, *eucharistia*, literally means "thanksgiving." It reflects the way in which when we delight in God—when we lean into gratitude—He gives us the desires of our heart; He grants us new vision. When we approach the table with gratitude for the gift, the gift achieves far more than simple bodily nourishment. Through the Eucharist, we are drawn again into the vision of our Lord, who longs not only to be present to us but for us to be present to Him. It is not a matter of whether Christ is with us; the Eucharist opens the eyes of our hearts again to recognize Jesus and participate in His life again.

By means of these two sacraments, Baptism and the Eucharist, all of us as Christians are given new contours for the shape of our lives. Through Baptism, we are awakened to the life of the Kingdom, a collective of people unified through the life of Jesus flowing in them by the power of the Holy Spirit. We are given eyes to see each other and the world around us in a way impossible with mere human eyes, and we are drawn into unity with each other. And through the Eucharist, we are called back to that unity continually and sustained by it. Through the overflowing gift of Christ in the world, through living signs taken from profoundly tangible elements of creation—water, bread, and wine—we see the world with eyes anew and are strengthened to enter back into it and hallow it through the power of Jesus in us.

And these signs are not meant to be merely experienced in a moment and then left behind as if a past memory, but continually lived out in and through the ordinary moments of our day-to-day existence.

Baptizing Imaginations

Before he became a Christian, C. S. Lewis's imagination was prepared for the peace and reconciliation he would eventually receive in Christianity through the writing of George MacDonald. Even though he didn't fully understand all the Christian imagery and analogy in MacDonald's *Phantastes*, the way MacDonald described the glory of the world enchanted him and set a small flame in Lewis's heart that would someday be fanned into the fire of a powerful faith that would change countless lives through his own writing. The way he described that experience is remarkable; he says, "my imagination was, in a certain sense, baptised."[15]

From the outflowing of MacDonald's vision of Christ in the creation and the way that entered into his writing, Lewis received a call to reconciliation with the reality from which he had become estranged, a reality that would soon become the enduring passion of his life. This is the power of the spirit of Baptism as it flows from the reality of our own participation in the sacrament of Baptism: Just as we have become initiated into the Kingdom and filled with the light of Christ, our lives, through every action we take in the world, might also be a potential signpost of the in-breaking Kingdom.

Madeleine L'Engle, in her book *Walking on Water*, discusses the unique way in which Christian artists take up this call to bear forth Christ's presence into the world. She describes the very tangible properties of art in its various forms as part and parcel of mediating Christ's presence: "to paint a picture or to write a story or to compose a song is an incarnational activity."[16] L'Engle turns to a very visceral metaphor to describe this process: "The artist is a servant who is willing to be a birth-giver. In a very real sense the artist (male or female) should be like Mary, who, when the angel told her that she was to bear the Messiah, was obedient to the command."[17] The connection is unmistakable: Artists who bear the presence of Christ in themselves are adjured to bear that witness in *incarnational* ways. Their artwork is sacramental in that it expresses the grace of God mediated through the stuff of the world. And though not all of us are artists, we are all called to this vocation of incarnation, whether through the astonishing refreshment of a cool drink or a warm meal, whether in the tenderhearted healing of the music which enters into the regular rhythms of our lives or the artwork we choose to display in our homes, whether in our willingness to witness to the glory of God in the bourgeoning beauty of spring or in the gift of kindness we give in an embrace. In every way we apply our senses to the work of beautifying the world, we have the opportunity to create instances of awakening to the bright light of the divine shining through all things. Every corner of our lives is drawn up into this calling: "There is nothing so secular that it cannot be sacred, and that is one of the deepest messages of the Incarnation."[18]

What we receive in the joy of the sacraments, we begin to see flowing out into the streams of our lives. Just as they mark the form of our lives of worship, those lines of practice begin to shape our everyday actions so that everything we do is immersed in the ethos of what these two sacraments represent: *reconciliation* to God's beautiful world and *sustenance* for the long journey within it. As we will discover in the coming pages, just as sacrament is the means by which we assign meaning through our hearts to that which we receive from the world itself, and then return back into the world in praise, our senses are the prime tools of that sacramental vocation. This sensory activity is the gospel at work, making known the Christ who has come into the world and sanctified it with His presence.

We are meant to do more than simply participate in the formal sacraments of the church. We are meant to become *living sacraments ourselves*, witnesses to the eternal King of the Kingdom to which we swear fealty. When we join our voices into that sacramental song, letting the dissonance of our old selves slip away and the new harmony of the Kingdom take hold in our hearts, we express in beautiful and lively form the person of Jesus to those most in need of Him.

Indeed, our work is more than simply converting souls, but rather opening people's eyes to the grand reality of the truly true, of a sacramental world which longs to reveal Jesus. We are to spend our lives transforming idols—dead ends which lead to sin and despair—into icons—windows through which the light of Christ shines. We are only able to do this if we reject the idolatry of our self-worship and allow ourselves to be transformed from the inside out. This is the work of sacraments and of the sacramental world within which they are placed: *that we ourselves are transformed from idols into icons.* Together, we become the living, palpable expression in our own time of the eternal reigning King, Jesus. We are being made into more than simply the gathering of the redeemed; through a sacramental world, and through the sacraments He has instituted for us, Jesus is transfiguring us, so that just as in His transfiguration, those who look at you and me and all that we do in our daily lives see the shining, beautiful, heavenly light of Christ breaking into their time and space.

COMMON SENSES

- Reflect on a recent church service that featured Baptism or Communion (or both). What images fill your mind as you think about those sacraments? What sensations do you recall? What made the expression of these sacraments different from the other aspects of the service?

- Think back to a favorite book or story from your childhood. What do you remember from its description of the world? What about the way it described the world captured your imagination? How might that story have shaped the way you relate to the world around you?

- Reflect on your own vocation. In what ways do you come closest to being a living sacrament in your daily work and rhythms? How does this discussion of the spirit of the sacraments cause you to think differently about your daily work and rhythms?

3

CHARGED WITH THE GRANDEUR

Beholding God's Glory in Nature

∼

Reading about nature is fine, but if a
person walks in the woods and listens carefully,
he can learn more than what is in books, for
they speak with the voice of God.

GEORGE WASHINGTON CARVER

I stepped off a cliff into the sickening emptiness of open air. What had been the firm ground of the knowledge of my future and my place in the world had suddenly been snatched out from under me, and I found myself in that split second of suspension before gravity does its work and begins its inescapable pull downward. In the still of my room, I sat paralyzed by my own dread, the gaping void of the unknown waiting to devour me. My heart crouched, huddled and hugging its knees in fearful sadness, not daring to look up and behold the vast meaninglessness that seemed to await me.

I shook my head to scatter away the shadows, even if just for a moment, and went through the motions of preparing to leave my little room; lacing my boots, making my bed, turning off the lights and locking the door. The dull ache of my own emptiness left me feeling half-conscious, as I dragged my feet down the stairs, along the hall, and out the door. As I shut it, I turned around to face the day.

My eyes strained to keep up with the persistence of brightness now bearing down on me. Even in the heavy gray of the half-clouded sky above, everything beneath burned with the chromatic potency of life. The jade of the verdant landscape around me cast itself into a shock of amber and scarlet in the leaves above me, defiantly wrestling to break free. All around, those which had already liberated themselves from the last desperate grasp of summer gathered in a gentle carpet under my clomping boots.

I pounded up steep inclines sheltered by shepherding trees, narrow entish guardians hovering watchfully above me. Over time, they would disperse, off to care for some other arboreal labor, leaving me out in the open of rolling green meadows. There, the wind whipped my hair and bit at my ankles, and the chafing cold seared my face with delicious fierceness. I pressed on, one foot in front of the other, until the rhythm began to draw away the fear, removing me from the void of my uncertainty and placing me in the immediacy of the here and now. In place of the ostinato of fears repeating themselves endlessly in my head, gentler melodies of birdsong and rippling water shooed the pounding rhythms away.

I marched on, until, at last, when I stopped and stood still, the silence no longer frightened me. Within it was not the violence of entropy, nor the terror of emptiness, but rather an overflowing stillness, a tranquility rooted in complete submersion.

The act of entering into nature with my sorrow and confusion, allowing those things to flow out into the dynamic life present in creation, brought me into the awareness, through nature's own image, that underneath the sheen of brokenness in the world is ever the in-breaking light of glory, remaking it day by day.

The Master Hand behind the Veil

Creation is the first frontier of the senses. Behind every sensory engagement we have in the world is the order and sensibility of the created world itself. Behind music, there is the harmonic resonance of sympathetic frequencies echoing in the melodious sounds of nature; behind visual art, there is the expressive multitude of colors, patterns, and figures at every level, from the cosmic down to the atomic; behind culinary inventiveness, the earth produces a bounty of nourishment more extravagant than the wildest of taste buds might imagine.

What we create and what we engage with creatively is always a response, an imitation flowing out of the creative activity already present in the warp and woof of the universe. This is because the whole of creation is the first act of creativity, the first and most primal work of art.

Nature bears the hallmarks of a creator whose cosmos isn't only orderly; it is beautiful. It is brought into being—and sustained—by the one who is the *image* of the invisible God. In this sense, it bears the imprint of God's image in its very form and flow. This vitality, this beauty, this structure and intention reveals to us something of God's nature, something of who He is. And this revelation of Himself through nature is meant to be grasped, to be understood, and to be responded to in praise. The beauty and the order of the universe are made manifest by the beholding of that glorious expression.

The pinnacle of God's creative act is the element within creation which sums up in itself the whole glorious interplay of the multiplicity of the cosmos beyond it: humanity. In each of us is the capacity to not only express the glory of creation, as part of the created order, but to offer it back in praise to God as the source of that glory.

Microcosms and Masterpieces

One of the prevailing concepts in the philosophy of the ancient world is the idea of microcosm and macrocosm. This concept describes the interplay between a small thing, a *micro*cosm, which fully expresses the essence of a much larger thing, the *macro*cosm. The microcosm is something that has all the same characteristics as its larger counterpart, but on a scale that can be more easily and readily understood. Many of the fathers of the church embraced this idea and integrated it into Christian thought. For them, the universe was the great macrocosm, which expressed in large scale the motions of God's activity in creation; and yet they envisioned humans as a microcosm of the universe. The fourth-century Cappadocian father Gregory of Nyssa imagined humans as an actual miniature cosmos in themselves. When humanity considers its own design, the beauty and structure and meaning in itself, its capacity to reason and to love and to experience goodness, it begins to comprehend, unlike any other aspect of creation, the larger work of God in the whole of the universe. According to the fathers, we are God's unique and summarizing expression of the artistry of creation.

Ephesians tells us "we are God's handiwork."[1] The Greek word for "handiwork" in this verse is *poiēma*. It is a version of the word *poiesis*, a concept in Greek philosophy which implies the bringing of something into existence which didn't exist before. A similar Latin term often used in the Christian tradition describes the way that God created the world *ex nihilo*—literally, "out of nothing."

When we as humans create something, our creative process is always referential of the world as we have experienced it. We cannot paint unless we use materials already in existence to portray colors and textures already present around us. We are able to make music only by ordering notes and rhythms according to the rules of consonance and dissonance, harmony and melody, already present in creation. When God creates, He does so with no reference point but Himself; everything that ever has been or ever will be comes from Him. The created world is imagination at its most infinitely pure, creativity at its most generative and expressive. Creation of the world *ex nihilo* is more than merely a task which God completes; it is His *magnum opus*, His *tour de force*.

It is no accident, then, that Paul uses the word *poiēma* to describe humans. For there is another essence of the word *poiesis*; it is what gives us our English word *poetry*. The New Living Translation expresses it a bit more directly: "We are God's *masterpiece*." The whole of the cosmos reveals the infinite creative genius of God as a poetic expression of His very nature; and humans are the ultimate triumph of that poem. Our capacity to know God through our senses is rooted not in an indulgent desire in ourselves but rather in the *plenitude*, the overflowing generosity, of a God who expresses His own image by creating the world and by designing us as the pinnacle of that creation. Our engagement with the tangible world is not meant to be something trivial but rather of the highest consequence. We are unique because, unlike the rest of the created order, we can comprehend creation as a beautiful work of art from the mind of God; and because of this, we are meant to engage with creation as an act of praise, returning the beauty and glory of creation to the one in whom it has its source.

This is how it should have been. And yet, a cursory glance at nature reveals that something has gone terribly wrong.

The Dearest Freshness behind the Veil

In the fifty-sixth canto from his long poem *In Memoriam A. H. H.*, Alfred Lord Tennyson reflected on the untimely death of his dear friend Arthur Hallam at only twenty-two.

Tennyson was deeply shaken by Hallam's death, and much of the poem questions the meaning of beauty and goodness in the face of the inevitable grief and sorrow that must also come into life. The fifty-sixth canto presses this sentiment into the realm of nature, where Tennyson examines human love and hope in light of the hard facts of nature's cycles of life and death. Nature herself speaks with icy finality of the countless "types," species who have disappeared in the massive extinction-level catastrophes of long-past geological history:

> She cries, "A thousand types are gone:
> I care for nothing, all shall go."[2]

Tennyson recognizes humans as the final creative expression of nature and wonders if their trust that love is "Creation's final law" will ultimately be fulfilled, when all the while nature screams a dire, contrasting message:

> Tho' Nature, red in tooth and claw
> With ravine, shriek'd against his creed.[3]

Tennyson wonders whether in the end, nature will have her way with humans, the finest and final creation, as with all the other multitude of species before them. He asks whether, when the end finally arrives, man will merely

> Be blown about the desert dust,
> Or seal'd within the iron hills?[4]

The answer eludes Tennyson; he doesn't give up hope entirely, but he leaves readers with only an ambiguous mystery just beyond his and our grasp:

> What hope of answer, or redress?
> Behind the veil, behind the veil.[5]

Whatever hope there is for Tennyson, it remains hidden beyond the "veil" of what nature presents to us. For him, all the beauty in the world is always dented and obscured by the intrusion of nature's brutal brokenness. Is Tennyson right about the fallenness of creation? Are we to accept his circumspection of nature?

Gerard Manley Hopkins gives a robust alternative vision in his poem "God's Grandeur." For Hopkins, Tennyson has it all backward. The thing to note is not that there is death, but rather that the beauty of the world is persistent and ever-present. Glory is the stubborn beating heart of the universe in turmoil. He describes this in vivid, electrifying verse:

> The world is charged with the grandeur of God.
>   It will flame out, like shining from shook foil;
>   It gathers to a greatness, like the ooze of oil
> Crushed. Why do men then now not reck his rod?[6]

Here, Hopkins suggests that humanity is not merely an innocent bystander or victim to nature's machinations, but that by not being mindful of God's glory in nature, humans participate in that spirit of destructiveness present in the universe. Likely reflecting on the rise of industrialism in his own time, Hopkins suggests that man covers the glory of nature with his "trade" and "toil," and that "the soil / Is bare now, nor can foot feel, being shod." And yet, somehow, even in spite of that ruinous spirit within humanity, nature gives us a vision of the persistence of beauty amid loss and brokenness:

> And for all this, nature is never spent;
>> There lives the dearest freshness deep down things.[7]

Hopkins makes an unassailable point: Nature is stubbornly full of vitality. We can see it all around us: It pulses out in powerful electromagnetic waves from quasars billions of miles from earth and in billowing waves beating against rocky shores. Countless blades of grass push up relentlessly through earth in an act of defiant life, and birds migrate year by year, birthing their young and returning in due season to their place of origin. As Tennyson so deftly weaves into his worrisome poetry, it is a common mantra in modern naturalism to discuss, in the most clinical and dry terms, the normality of death in the narrative of nature, the regularity of extinction of species, and yet what of the way in which, as Hopkins suggests, life springs forth anew, in equally countless ways, all over again? What are we to do with this persistence? Which image do we accept: that nature is "red in tooth and claw," and is fundamentally full of darkness and death, or that "There lives the dearest freshness deep down things," and that nature is ultimately beautiful and resilient? Perhaps the answer is as complex as the struggle in our own human hearts, the struggle to overcome sin and death and embrace grace instead. Perhaps both Tennyson's and Hopkins's stories are telling the truth at the same time and the key to understanding how to grapple with this mystery is hidden within ourselves.

Nature and Grace

In Terrence Malick's magnificent film *Tree of Life*, two narratives are presented on a grand scale, intertwined with each other: the narrative of nature, as represented by the story of the universe itself, unraveled in grand sequences of nebulas and galaxies swirling into existence and epochs of great emergence and destruction of species; and the narrative of grace, as mediated by moments of transcendent beauty throughout the film. Light streams through water or filters through flittering leaves on a tree; a woman dances with such joy that her feet lift off the ground for the hint of a moment. These metanarratives are threaded into the story of a midcentury American family in Waco, Texas. It is, in some ways, a quintessential story, as ubiquitous as sun and rain: a hardworking father striving to provide for his family; a loving mother trying to seek the good of her children and honor her husband; two sons, in friendship and competition with each other and in fear and curiosity of their father.

Quickly, the cosmic threads of nature and grace begin to

appear, woven into the day-to-day of the smaller story, and at first, they play their part according to a preordained understanding: Nature is cold and unforgiving; it was begun in chaotic, explosive fire, is sustained by merciless destruction, and presses on relentlessly toward a whimpering end with a dead earth and a dying sun. Grace, is, on the other hand, transcendent, otherworldly, caught up in a spiritual transfiguration of the material world. Certain characters seem to be associated with the former narrative, and others with the latter. One of the family members muses: "Nature only wants to please itself. Get others to please it too. Likes to lord it over them. To have its own way. It finds reasons to be unhappy when all the world is shining around it. And love is smiling through all things."[8] It is as if we as viewers are to understand that the created world is broken and dark, and that only in transcending it and engaging in the otherworldly, ethereal life of grace can we overcome it.

It is only later that the viewer begins to realize that the narratives of nature and grace may not be mutually exclusive, and it is the characters themselves who draw the lines so firmly. One character gives us a hint toward this: "Help each other. Love everyone. Every leaf. Every ray of light. Forgive."[9] It is in the eye of the beholder that nature becomes either cold and cruel or transcendent; the impetus is on us. Another character quotes nearly verbatim from Fyodor Dostoyevsky's *The Brothers Karamazov*: "I wanted to be loved because I was great . . . I'm nothing. Look at the glory around us: trees, birds. I lived in shame. I dishonored it all, and didn't notice the glory."[10] The narrative of grace is there for the taking in nature, but we are the mediators of how we receive it. Nature becomes a mirror of our inner selves. If *The Tree of Life* is right, the way we engage with the interplay between beauty and brokenness in nature will largely be determined by the way we engage with the beauty and brokenness of ourselves, through our encounter with grace. Nature, in other words, is a lot like us. Nature, as Saint Francis tells us, is our *sister*.

To Practice Resurrection

Saint Francis had a penchant for the glory of the world and God's presence and movement within it. In a time of upheaval and change in the church, when spirituality had strayed from its dedication to the simplicity of the gospel, Saint Francis began multiple monastic orders based on a rule of poverty and a rejection of material things, in emulation of Christ. In part, this rejection of worldly desires was not an eschewing of the created world itself but, in a sense, was actually drawn from Francis's love of creation and his awareness of the glory already given by God through nature. He believed that like us, nature is tainted by sin and in need of redemption, but that also like us, nature is made to praise God.

In his beautiful "Canticle of Brother Sun," Saint Francis praises God for the way in which various aspects of creation express the image of God and return their praise back to Him. In each instance, Saint Francis refers to these created elements as "brothers" or "sisters":

> Praised be You, my Lord, with all your creatures,
> especially Sir Brother Sun,
> Who is the day and through whom You give us light.
> And he is beautiful and radiant with great splendour;
> and bears a likeness of You, Most High One.[11]

Notice the way in which Francis not only praises the sun because of its beauty but attributes that beauty to the divine likeness of Jesus imprinted within that sublimity. In this way, Francis uses the elegance of the poetry to heighten our awareness of the way in which nature expresses that image. He goes on to praise God for the earth as well, cleverly retitling mother earth as "Sister Mother Earth."[12] In this way, he affirms the ancient understanding of the earth as that from which we draw sustenance to live day to day; and yet like us, the earth has its ultimate beginning in the Father, who is over both and over all.

But then, in an abrupt, surprising shift, Francis turns to an aspect of nature seemingly incompatible with the goodness of God, an aspect which, as we have already seen, Tennyson feared above all things: death. Just like the sun and moon, or the elements of wind and water and fire, death, according to Francis, is also our sibling:

> Praised be You, my Lord, through our Sister Bodily Death,
> from whom no living man can escape. . . .
> Blessed are those whom death will find in Your most holy will,
> for the second death shall do them no harm.[13]

What Francis expresses here is a glorious, universal truth of the gospel: Death, for the Christian, is merely the prologue to resurrection, for just as Christ passed through death and was raised again into new life, so our journey through death brings us into that life with Him. And yet by integrating our death as an element of the created world that participates in revealing God's goodness to us, Francis shows how our victory over death is not merely our victory but the victory of God's action "to reconcile to himself all things, whether things on earth or things in heaven, by making peace through his blood, shed on the cross,"[14] as we've already heard from Colossians. When we who are redeemed in Christ recognize the appearance of death in nature, it no longer acts as a statement of finality, but rather a vivid image of the desire for all things to be made new.

Paul tells us that "all creation has been groaning as in the pains of childbirth right up to the present time."[15] This is a beautiful thought, that nature is destined for some sort of redemption as well. And yet, how could we possibly know that this is true? From what source are we to draw our hope that creation will be redeemed? Paul makes it clear for us: "And we believers also groan, even though we have the Holy Spirit within us as a foretaste of future glory, for we long for our bodies to be released from sin and suffering."[16] Our bodies, as participants in the created world, given to spiritual and physical corruption, long to be restored; and if our bodies, as part of that world, are destined for restoration, then so also must the world in which they now exist be brought back into glory.

Resurrection is not simply a nice, abstract idea, but rather a truth-telling event which has *already occurred in the fabric of the world itself* and continues to foreshadow our future destiny. To believe in resurrection of the body means to believe that the world in which our bodies exist in the present time will, in some way, be restored and recreated, just like us. Not only can we not ignore nature; it is the very space which is given to us as a way to *imagine resurrection*.

Nature gives us, writ large, a vision of the complexity of our own desire for participation in God; our fall from grace and the corruption that comes with sin; and the persistence of beauty, order, and goodness—just as we, as humans, ever bear the image of God as an imprint on our very essences. It, like us, longs for the day in which it will be made whole once more by the one who brought it into being at the beginning. Nature is the cosmic canvas of the drama of sin and redemption, groaning, not unlike us, for the final moment when Christ will restore all things to perfect participation in God. In nature, we cannot extract the fallenness of the world from the fact that somehow, amid natural disasters and illness and the recurrence of death, we are ever confronted with beauty, order, structure, *cosmos*. Nature forces us to hold these things together in tension, by means of the only way that we can possibly bear such a tension: through our sensory perception. Like Jacob wrestling with the angel, we must cast ourselves headlong into the turbulent swirl of the unknowable, entering into creation exactly as we know that it is through our encounter of it; neither what we wish it might be in our wildest imaginations nor given fully to the chaos of our worst dreams but rather the truthfulness of what it speaks to us through each tangible point of contact. We must grasp it until the knuckles of our senses are white with strain, and declare to it what Jacob shouted to his angelic counterpart: "I will not let you go unless you bless me."[17] In this way, we will be woven into the pattern of creation's weave which, like us, is broken and yet longs for renewal in Christ, longs to return to the one in whom it has its source and be restored to glory once more. If we are faithful to persistently embrace nature, to seek the glory and grace in the midst of its imperfection and confusion, somehow, we will find hidden within it what Tolkien called *eucatastrophe*: the sudden joy at the end of a long sorrow. In our embrace of nature and its persistent beauty, we will receive a powerful, sensory encounter with the work of the resurrected one, who is turning back the tide of darkness. In our embrace of nature, our sighs for deliverance will be given resonance through the cry of the whole universe itself to be reborn in newness of life once more.

Created for Good Works

Every day is a choice between reactively resigning to the seeming entropy around us or proactively willing ourselves to see the creative glory at hand. The stakes are very high; seeing the glory isn't simply a passive recognition of something beautiful but instead an active willingness to participate. Giving in to despair is the passive act; it is resignation to being consumed. Beholding the glory of nature doesn't mean ignoring the darkness. Rather, it is the willingness to participate in the creative bearing of light *into* darkness. Darkness has no power in itself; the static void of darkness shrivels in the presence of dynamic light. When we allow ourselves to enter into the midst of nature and behold the persistent glory amid the confusion and the despair, we take up arms as co-creators collaborating in the imaginative re-creation of all things.

In our earlier conversation about Ephesians, we discovered that we are God's *poīēma*, his "masterpiece." We are created to recognize God's beauty, order, and goodness in the grand scope of creation and in ourselves. And as the pinnacle of God's creative work, we have the capacity to respond to that recognition by offering up our participation in the world as worship to God. But there is a second element to that verse, just after Paul's vibrant statement about God's creative work in us, that gives us understanding of *how* to offer up that participation: "For we are God's masterpiece. *He has created us anew in Christ Jesus, so we can do the good things he planned for us long ago.*"[18] We are living poems, created in a world of poetic expression, and though we, and the world with us, become cut off from the grace of that poetry through our sin, in Christ, we are restored to the beauty of verse. We are invited once more into the ongoing *poiesis* which has never ceased in God's activity, but which, in Jesus, we are able to enter into once more. And just as through us, sin came into the world, through Jesus, we are called to repoeticize the world anew.

This is what Tolkien referred to as "sub-creation." For Tolkien, our engagement with the sensory aspects of the world—especially through using those sensory aspects as expression in music, story, and other forms of artistry—is our participation in the redemptive creativity of God in restoring the world. When we create or imagine, when we sing or write or paint or even craft a delicious meal, we are acting as sub-creators, allowing God to work His creative restoration through us. Tolkien says it this way in his essay "On Fairy Stories":

> Every sub-creator, wishes in some measure to be a real maker, or hopes that he is drawing on reality: hopes that the peculiar quality of this secondary world (if not all the details) are derived from Reality, or are flowing into it.... The peculiar quality of the 'joy' in successful Fantasy can thus be explained as a sudden glimpse of the underlying reality or truth.[19]

In other words, the way we express creativity in the world is meant to be drawn from God's redemptive activity already at work in and through that creation. All the tools of our participation in God's restoration are already given to us in nature, from the musicality of a symphonic cosmos to the proportion and elegance of color, texture, and form in the natural world around us. We are called to use each of those tools to understand our own participation in restoration, in sub-creation. In these coming chapters, we will explore many of these elements and consider how we might engage with them and understand them, so that we might participate in the life of sub-creation, acting as the hands and feet of God's redemptive work in the world. We begin our exploration in the next chapter, with music.

COMMON SENSES

- Take a walk anywhere there is a natural bit of green: a park, a botanical garden, an arboretum, a hiking trail, an orchard, a forest, a beach. Before you depart, ask God to open your senses to observe His presence. Take a notepad and pen with you, and as you walk, describe your sensory experiences. What colors do you see? What do you smell? What sounds are around you? What interesting textures are nearby, and what do they feel like? Perhaps you'll even come across something to taste!

- At some point in your walk, find somewhere to sit quietly and observe the world around you for a few minutes. Answer the following questions: During your time at rest, did you see or hear or observe anything that surprised you? Did you experience anything that made you feel unsettled? Was there anything that delighted you?

- If you are able during your moment of observation (or if not, after you have finished your walk), offer up a prayer and express to God the various things you experienced; ask Him to help you know His grace in those experiences and to have an eye to recognize His presence in your experience of nature.

4

CREATION'S SONG

Experiencing God's Presence in Music

⌒

Music expresses that which cannot be said and
on which it is impossible to be silent.

VICTOR HUGO

It was with hushed anticipation that we all filed out of the noise and bustle of go-home traffic in the center of London into the awaiting performance auditorium. There is something unique about Royal Albert Hall that always invokes a sense of the impending arrival of something meaningful, but that night, among the many gathered there, a deeper stillness pressed outward past elegant attire and smiles of the audience. They held it in the quietude of their faces, in the hush of their voices. Even before the Tallis Scholars walked out onto the stage to begin their performance, there was a solemnity in the crowd, a corporate understanding, even without the experience of the music to come, of what it was we had gathered to commemorate.

The lights went down and the hush became a silence pregnant with expectation. Out of that silence, music began to rise up. A warm, harmonious bed of suspended strings wafted into the awaiting space, gracing us like a gentle wind, and then was gone just as quickly, the stillness returning as if a question. Suddenly into the emptiness of that query rushed an astonishing and pointillistic shout: *Fos.* The Greek word for light. As quick as it came, it was gone. Once again the strings rose up, but were being transformed; dissonance began to enter into this new sonic soundscape, a subtle but powerful wayward line breaking into the serenity of the original sound bed. Again, as if defiantly pushing into the confusion, the harmonious and jubilant declaration of *fos* reverberated into the awaiting space, as if to render the dissonance as nothingness, unable to touch the vibrance of what was stated. Again and again the dance of discordance and consonance tumbled in the open space of the auditorium, a dramatic and mesmerizing battle of the bright and unmoving voices against the ever-morphing, increasingly strident tones of the strings underneath, until finally the light became suffusive, covering all and filling the space with extravagant mystery and infinitude. This was not a light which comes and goes, a fleeting dance of luminance that alights on us and flits away. This was the light of heaven, the light in which God dwells, the radiance which Saint Paul says in 1 Timothy 6:16 is "so brilliant that no human can approach him." It is this light, this inaccessible brightness, which could burn us away into ash without a second thought, that somehow, through the invocation of the Holy Spirit, might somehow dwell within us. A light shining in the darkness, which the darkness could not comprehend. It was this light which was invoked, a light rooted in *doxa*—glory—a light with which every heart in that room that night pleaded to make itself real in each of us.

Because this was no ordinary night. This was August 4, 2014, exactly one hundred years to the day, the hour, the very minute, of England's declaration of war against Germany. We were there to recall the darkness of four bloody, brutal years, a time in which the world descended into chaos and confusion, a time when it seemed like light might be extinguished and lost forever, buried under the mud and muck of death and destruction.

Into such an impossible, harrowing vision of the world, light was invoked, testing the endurance of such a potent darkness. And it was a palpable darkness indeed; for when those moments of music had finally completed their opening declaration of glory, an actor somberly walked on stage and intoned the words of the British foreign secretary in 1914, Sir Edward Grey, as he reflected on impending war: "The lamps are going out all over Europe. We shall not see them lit again in our lifetime."[1]

And then, all over the room, the house lights truly were extinguished, and darkness fell on us all. Never before and never since have I experienced such a complete silence in a room with so many people; it was a silence born not simply of the civic reverence of a people who have a profound sense of their own history, as the English often do. It was born of the immediacy of the darkness in our own hearts, of the continued presence of discord, grief, and sadness that linger in countless ways in our own time and in our own lives. Yes, we had been captured by the invocation of light, but the darkness had rendered us speechless, unable to open our lips, waiting for an answer.

It was into that oppressive, enduring silence that new music began to ring out:

Little lamb, who made thee
Dost thou know who made thee[2]

The simple, gentle words from William Blake's mystical poem "The Lamb" were jarring; not only as a seemingly meager response to such a spectacularly heavy impingement of evil and despair but also because the music itself was suffused with discordance. Somehow, it perfectly encased our sense of confusion, of suspense, but not because we had succumbed to the dark. Rather, because in the midst of that interwoven darkness and gentleness, we were recalled to the light that had only so recently been extinguished. In this music was the encounter with a Lamb who, by taking our disharmony and dissonance unto Himself, walked into the midst of our darkness and brought us light, brought us consonance and beauty. Out of the Lamb's radical self-giving dissonance we would receive the consonance of resolution light, which had been planted in the soil of our hearts.

As each voice began to intertwine with every other part, somewhere in the room, a candle was lit. And then suddenly it was on us all, a soft and yet defiant luminance, daring us to flare out against the darkness.

And in the intertwining of that painful, illuminated music with the gathered shadow of dark, we knew that nothing could extinguish that fragile light.

Somehow, what had been mere harmony had become a word that spoke beyond our own capacity to communicate. The candlelight was the shining proof of what the music had done in our hearts. When we all walked out of that space into the nighttime of London, each of us was lit with the fire, the Holy Light, burning within our souls.

You see, on that evening in London it was not enough to simply know of light. On a night of such challenging remembrance, we needed more than to simply be told that the light was real; we needed to experience it. Music had taken mere words, static expressions of things like light and lambs, and sanctified them. It had moved our spirits beyond simply assenting to an idea, a concept, and had infused each concept with meaning, with a truth unspeakable in words alone. Each person in the auditorium that evening knew intellectually of the existence of light, but in the face of what we were to walk through, we needed that light to be made manifest in us. And it was breath, just like the breath of the Holy Spirit, the light bringer, which shouted out the harmonies that buried themselves deep in our souls, planting the light as a promise. We weren't simply told of the light; we were made participants in it through an utterance deeper than words. And when we were in the midst of our descent into darkness, waiting in silence, longing for that light to take on form and become a comfort to us, it was music which made the Lamb, *our* Lamb, real and palpable. *Who made thee. . .*[3] The dissonance made that question all the more urgent in the confusion of darkness, and when the answer truly came, it showed us the truth: *We are called by his name.*[4] Together with the whole consecrated crowd gathered there, I raised my candle against the darkness.

This is the power of music; music operates in the world of encounter, which moves us past observers and invites us to become participants. Inherent within music is the knowledge that some truths are not communicable simply through words but must instead be encountered. Words are certainly able to plant the seed of truth deep in the soil of our hearts, but music animates the seed of truth buried within us and causes it to grow. In our most meaningful moments in life, we use music to imbue the ideas we intend to communicate with meaning. We have requiem music for funerals and wedding marches for marriage ceremonies; many of us know "Reveille" and "Taps" by heart, or other similar tunes in civic music, and merely hearing the beginning strains of our national anthem might cause us to instinctively stand or draw our hands to our hearts. Music has that much power to invoke our passions, our affections. Music gives expression to the inner voice that is unable to communicate through spoken word and articulates a spiritual landscape that we believe in by default but often find challenging to make real in our lives.

The Hymn of the Cosmos

The fourth-century Cappadocian bishop and church father Gregory of Nyssa had a special relationship with music. For Gregory, like many of the other church fathers we discussed in the last chapter, the whole universe is tantalizingly filled to the brim with the presence and activity of Christ. And Gregory took that cosmic view even further: For him, the whole of creation is a hymn sung in praise to the Trinity and is conducted by God Himself. Gregory saw in the vastness of creation's variety and expression a single unity, how out of the multitude of moving pieces in nature, there is a grand whole. Just like how an orchestra made up of dozens upon dozens of different instruments and performers still performs a single symphonic piece together under the baton of the maestro conductor at its center, so, too, the universe, in all its multiplicity and diversity, is drawn together into a unified glory. For Gregory, the dynamic movement of the whole cosmos is "a musical harmony which produces a blended and marvelous hymn of the power which controls the universe."[5] In other words, the very warp and woof of the fabric of the cosmos is expressed to us as something melodious, something lyrical; something *musical*. The whole of nature is a *song*. And not only that; as those who understand and can see, who can hear and respond to that song, our purpose as humans is to take up that song in praise. We are made *to be musical*.

Just like the other fathers, Gregory engages with the concept of microcosm and macrocosm, small things that are the perfect miniature image of a much larger thing, but for Gregory, this concept only makes sense through the lens of the musical. We are able to engage with the divine through music because the music we create and listen to as humans participates as a small part of the vast music of the cosmos itself, conducted by God. If the universe is fundamentally musical, then humans, who are a microcosm of the universe, are themselves made specifically for music. For Gregory, not only are the whole of our bodies made for singing; he thinks of the human body like an instrument. Our windpipe is like a flute, our palates like "the bridge of the lyre"[6] (an ancient harplike instrument). We are custom-made to praise God. Hans Boersma says this about Gregory's vision: "the purpose of life, according to Gregory, is to make music."[7]

It is perhaps not surprising, then, that in the Christian community around Gregory in fourth-century Cappadocia, hymns of praise appeared for the first time, hymns which have lasted the ages and which many churches still include in their regular worship today. These hymns were written for morning and evening prayer and expressed the goodness of God through His creation, juxtaposing the light of creation with the light of Christ, at the very hours when the illumination of the sun arrived with the morning or gave way to evening lamplight. The title of the hymn written for evening prayer betrays this underlying message of luminance: "O Gladsome Light." The text, as translated and repeated in the Book of Common Prayer, unveils the glorious interplay between divine and creational light:

O gracious Light,
pure brightness of the everliving Father in heaven,
O Jesus Christ, holy and blessed!

Now as we come to the setting of the sun,
and our eyes behold the vesper light,
we sing thy praises, O God: Father, Son, and Holy Spirit.[8]

For these early believers, the hymn of Vespers was the centerpiece of their evening prayer. The music of worship became the way to respond to the music of the cosmos masterfully brought into being through Christ. In singing this hymn of praise at the hour of the lighting of the lamps, ancient Christians like Gregory participated in a profound and transformative understanding of music's power: When we engage with music, both through listening to it and participating in its beauty by producing it, we resonate with the song which God is singing in and through the universe. Music draws our whole selves upward into the song of all creation, conducted by God Himself.

Bridging the Eternal Divide

Music is a connective tissue between our earthly, tangible lives and the intangible movement of the divine in and through all things. As the late poet and philosopher John O'Donohue said:

> There is something deeper still in the way that music pervades us. In contrast to every other art form, it finds us out in a more immediate and total way. . . . It is as though music reaches that subtle threshold within us where the soul dovetails with the eternal.[9]

Music acts as a vital pathway into the participation of the eternal reality beyond our own, the eternal reality which so evades us when we try to get our minds around it. It delves into the heart of both our deepest longing and the paradoxical fear of the unknown caught up in that longing. We know that in Christ, we are restored to participation in God's life, and we are destined to be resurrected into eternal life in God's presence. And yet, how do we, in our finite bodies, and with our limited intellects, begin to grasp the incomprehensibility of the eternal, divine word of Christ, begotten of His Father before all ages, who entered into our time, took on our flesh, emptied Himself of His unbounded heavenly glory, and inhabited a fragile, finite human body?

The fear of the unknown contained in the concept of

eternity is one which visits many of us even in our child-hood. We know that we fervently want to live on, but we can't imagine what it could possibly be like to live without end; embedded in our fragile bodies is the instinctual aware-ness of the toll that injury and illness and age will exact on us. The very thought of such an eternity, apprehended purely through our intellect, does not comfort us but makes us tremble with fear. Our finite minds cannot grasp what they cannot imagine, and the eternal is not in the purview of the human mind; it remains hidden away in our hearts. As Ecclesiastes says, "He has planted eternity in the human heart, but even so, people cannot see the whole scope of God's work from beginning to end."[10] In our very essence is an eternity which our bodies and minds are not able to understand. Our rational thought can only take us so far until we reach the precipice of the edge of that which is ana-lytically comprehendible. Beyond that is the darkness where our minds cannot go; only something beyond our intellect itself can possibly be our guide.

Our hearts, remember, are engines of sacrament. They take mere information and assign meaning to that rational knowledge, giving us the capacity to recognize God's pres-ence in the world and respond to it in praise and participa-tion. Of course, at the very core of the sacramental world is Christ Himself, through whom the whole world was created; by whose incarnation, death, and resurrection the world was redeemed; and in whom the world is destined to be restored when Christ reconciles all things to Himself. The longing of our heart to participate in the sacramental reality which imbues the whole of creation is never a vague engagement with an unnamed divine presence but rather an encounter with the person of Jesus, the bridge between the human and the divine. Jesus is the one through whom we have access to the fullness of life in God, who recovers us from our sin and fallenness and restores us to life in the Father.

When we take Christ into our lives, His presence awakens the hidden gift of the eternal written on our hearts. To walk with Christ is not simply to assent to the idea of who He is but to experience His life restoring ours and reorienting the eyes of our hearts to His heavenly reality. O'Donohue believed this is precisely the liminal space which music fills and gives meaning:

> We always seem to forget that the soul has two faces.
> One face is turned towards our lives; it animates and
> illuminates every moment of our presence. The other face
> is always turned towards the divine presence. . . . Perhaps
> this is where the mystical depth of music issues from: that
> threshold where the face of the soul becomes imbued
> with the strange tenderness of divine illumination.[11]

In other words, music acts as a sort of connective tissue between the truth of the eternal hidden in our hearts and our engagement with the tangible world around us. Music becomes a way for us to contemplate Jesus, to understand, even without being able to articulate in words, even in the limitations of our finite form, what it means to be *in Christ* and to anticipate the heavenly reality that He has made possible through Himself. The Jesus that we invite into the fabric of our lives is the eternal reigning King over all creation, transcendent in heavenly majesty at the right hand of His father yet close at hand to us. As Hebrews tells us, Jesus is even now "in the place of honor at the right hand of the majestic God in heaven";[12] and yet this is the same Jesus who walked the roads of earth, held human hands, touched and healed countless hurting people. That same Christ is in each of us, and in Him, the eternal reality which Ecclesiastes says is hidden in our hearts is animated and brought to life. First Peter expresses the joy of this truth: "Now we live with great expectation, and we have a priceless inheritance—an inheritance that is kept in heaven for you, pure and undefiled, beyond the reach of change and decay."[13] Though we live in a broken place, a world not yet restored, we know that we are destined for redemption, for the remaking of all things and the rising into life eternal in Christ. Music assists us in comprehending the joy of what our finite, flawed minds cannot yet understand, allowing us to engage in the sacramental knowledge of the already-and-not-yet of our eternal future in Christ. It accomplishes this by affectively drawing us into an awareness of that glory beyond mere intellectual understanding. Music enables us, as Peter says, to "rejoice with a glorious, inexpressible joy."[14]

Messiaen's Music of Heavenly Stillness

Like many of his time, Olivier Messiaen, the great twentieth-century French composer, found himself caught up in the turmoil of World War II. In what surely must have seemed like the end of the world, while interned in a German prisoner-of-war camp, Messiaen wrote what would be later recognized as his compositional masterpiece, *Quartet for the End of Time*. Though written in bleak surroundings during a time of great darkness, *Quartet* is hardly a hopeless work, but instead celebrates the longing for the completion of all things in Jesus at the end of time, when we will forever behold the eternal Christ with our eyes unveiled. In two particular movements, "Praise to the Eternity of Jesus" and "Praise to the Immortality of Jesus," Messiaen writes expansive, tranquil soundscapes of piano and string. In the latter, the effervescent violin melody is gradually gathered with a heartbeat-like piano accompaniment upward toward a high note, which gently and peacefully then fades into pure silence. This is what Messiaen wrote of the moment:

> Why this second eulogy? It addresses more specifically the second aspect of Jesus: Jesus the Man, the Word made flesh, immortally resurrected, to impart us his life. This movement is pure love. The progressive ascent toward the extremely high register represents the ascension of man toward his Lord, of the son of God toward his Father, of deified Man toward Paradise.[15]

Messiaen uses the emotive power of music to draw the listener close to the ascent of the incarnate Christ into heaven, taking them on a journey through the world of their experience that mere intellectual grasping toward the idea of eternity cannot achieve. Messiaen uses his music to awaken in the hearts of his listeners the longing for the eternal peace which will someday be ours in Christ, even though we remain caught in the struggles and strains of our earthly circumstances.

The first performance was in the internment camp itself, with both guards and prisoners in the audience. Etienne Pasquier, a fellow inmate of Messiaen's and the cellist for that premiere performance—as well as an agnostic—described the scene during the performance, resorting to spiritual vocabulary to describe it: "Everyone listened reverently, with an almost religious respect, including those who perhaps were hearing chamber music for the first time. It was 'miraculous.'"[16] Through music, Messiaen transported a disparate audience filled with people at enmity with each other to a heavenly space, in contemplation of Christ. Music overcame the limitations of the circumstances of the world in which Messiaen's work emerged, a world of brokenness and despair, and provoked an awareness of the eternal in-breaking of Christ's heavenly peace.

And just as music can transport us into the heights of a divine awareness beyond our capacity to rationally grasp, so, too, does the extent of its reach go as far downward into our human experience as it does upward into divine life. It descends into our most potent troubles and sorrows and hallows them by illuminating the presence of Christ, the God who has suffered, and who is most present to us in our most profound sufferings.

Out of the Depths

The Scottish composer James MacMillan has often engaged with the theme of divine presence and suffering in his concert music. His compositions are often filled with challenging dissonances and tumultuous passages, even when—or perhaps especially when—writing music themed around Jesus and His incarnation. He describes why this is:

> Music is the most spiritual of the arts. More than the other arts, I think, music seems to get into the crevices of the human-divine experience. Music has the power to look into the abyss as well as to the transcendent heights. It can spark the most severe and conflicting extremes of feeling and it is in these dark and dingy places where the soul is probably closest to its source where it has its relationship with God, that music can spark life that has long lain dormant.[17]

For MacMillan, the capacity of music to express the full scope of the collective of human emotion means that it can draw transcendence into the midst of our immanent struggles and sadnesses. The profound story hidden in the depths of

Jesus's life is that the joy of His resurrection emerges from the total extent of darkness over which He claims victory. In His suffering on the cross, God Himself enters into our abandonment, our most excruciating moments, our darkest and loneliest experiences, and meets us there. When we are in our worst moments, that is when the incarnation of Jesus is most profoundly expressed, for there is no depth which God will not enter to be with us, to comfort us with His presence.

Much of MacMillan's musical world is built around this singular idea; when he writes music themed around Christ and His incarnation, he most often does it in the sonic vernacular of troubled rhythmic clashes and distressing cacophony. In this way, his music reveals to us through our affective experience that God is "close to the brokenhearted,"[18] as the Psalms tell us, and that Jesus, the man "acquainted with deepest grief,"[19] is the revealed expression of the God who loves us and entered into our most difficult experiences.

Even in his most exquisite music, this idea finds rooting in the way in which it challenges his performers, pushing their voices further to produce that beauty. His Strathclyde Motets, a collection of short choral pieces which he wrote to be accessible to church choirs, are often centered on the theme of Christ as a light entering our world. One of his most popular motets from the collection, *O Radiant Dawn*, has words which bear a striking resemblance to the *Phos Hilaron*, words taken and translated from an early Christian chant, the "O Oriens":

O Radiant Dawn,
  splendor of eternal light, sun of justice:
  come and shine on those who dwell in darkness and in the
  shadow of death.[20]

And yet, though the words are numinous, and the music equally so, he shares how he wanted the pieces to still challenge and push their performers, to help them understand the genuine reality of the incarnation, coming to us in the very midst of the grittiness and struggle of our earthly existence: "There has to be a sense of physical graft involved in the most spiritual of music . . . It has to be physically intense."[21] MacMillan doesn't want us to miss the costliness of glory, the way in which it reveals the full consequence of Jesus's incarnation. Perhaps it is not surprising, then, that a work as transcendent as "O Radiant Dawn," a composition themed around light, was written for liturgical use on the shortest day of the year, December 21st. Perhaps it reveals to us that even in our dimmest of days, Christ is with us, as John 1 says: "The light shines in the darkness, and the darkness can never extinguish it."[22] By writing glorious harmonies which require serious concentration and effort to produce, MacMillan uses his music to evoke the *sense* of incarnation through the human body itself, allowing its singers to *feel* the meaning of Christ's incarnation even beyond simply receiving it as a theological idea. MacMillan shows how music speaks the sacramental language of the eternal through our finite bodies, the transcendence of glorious melodies and interwoven harmonies produced by lungs limited by the shortness of breath and the constraint of straining muscles.

The Breathless Infinite

Gregory of Nyssa was right, then: We are made to make music, our bodies intricately designed to sing in praise. And yet, rather than merely praising the utility of our constructed selves, perhaps it is in the very limitations of our form that music opens up the beauty of God's infinite reality: our constant need to breathe in and out again and again, the challenge to stay in tune and on beat, the frailty of our voices, so easily susceptible to injury or illness. It is a gift given precisely through the constraints of our bodies. As 2 Corinthians says of Christ in us, "we have this treasure in earthen vessels, so that the surpassing greatness of the power will be of God and not from ourselves."[23] God uses the earthen vessels of our limited selves to express the limitlessness of the goodness awaiting us beyond the veil of our earthly lives. Somehow, paradoxically, the more our limitations come into view, the more God's power is expressed.

In his song "Saturn," the lead singer of Sleeping at Last, Ryan O'Neal, remembers a conversation with a dying friend, who, even as they face the final veil, wants to reflect on the persistence of beauty and light:

> you taught me the courage of stars before you left.
> how light carries on endlessly, even after death.

with shortness of breath, you proclaimed the infinite.
how rare and beautiful it is to even exist.[24]

O'Neal describes the difficulty in fully comprehending the extent of his friend's words, longing to grasp what is beyond reach:

i couldn't help but ask
for you to say it all again
i tried to write it down
but i could never find a pen

In the second verse, O'Neal repeats for himself what he has already observed of his friend, transforming the meaning of the words:

with shortness of breath, i'll explain the infinite—
how rare and beautiful it truly is that we exist.

And then . . . the lyric ends. Right in the middle of the second verse, the whole of the effervescent scene is drawn to an abrupt and unexpected close. In one sense, the listener might think they are being given an experience of the suddenness of our ending, how quickly it can quench the flame of our existence.

And yet, there's more to the picture. Bookending O'Neal's singing are long stretches of glorious, instrumental soundscapes invoking images of cosmic splendor and celestial beauty.

In a sense, the limitations of O'Neal's human expression are, through music, carried upward into the transcendence of an infinite glory. O'Neal's song shows how music makes evident to us, through the restraints of our human experience in bringing it to bear, the words which Jesus speaks over us through Paul: "My grace is all you need. My power works best in weakness."[25] As Paul says in the same chapter, "I am glad to boast about my weaknesses, so that the power of Christ can work through me. . . . For when I am weak, then I am strong."[26]

Our human frailty and limitations are the space in which Christ brings about good things through us, not because we are strong but because He is. Music gives us a way to imaginatively enter into this reality, to experience the beauty that can result from our willingness to put our limited bodies in the service of expression. In music, we communicate with the vocabulary of a sacramental participation in God's life in the world itself, and when we reach the limits of our capacity to express what we can understand, music speaks the words beyond our understanding.

A Living Improvisation

The brilliant jazz pianist Bill Evans was known as a master of improvisation. From his solo keyboard sounds, drawing enlivened melodies and arpeggios seemingly out of thin air, to his genius capacity to effortlessly receive melodic ideas from his collaborators and develop them in real time, Evans's music sang with the brilliance of the unexpected.

One of his most famous works is entitled "Peace Piece." Recorded in 1958 in one sitting at the very end of a long recording session, the composition of the work is made up of the same two chords repeated in the same ostinato, or short theme, over and over through to the very end. The sound bed of that ostinato is tranquil and gentle, almost pastoral. Over it, Evans improvises what begins as a light, open, suspended line in his right hand. At first, the ad-libbed melody is bright and relaxed, well attuned to the repeated rhythm underneath it. And then, over time, it begins to morph. At first it grows momentarily more spirited, then backs away, as if not able to fully emerge. This dance of procession and return continues for a while until, almost without notice, Evans introduces a little dissonance, like a splash in water which becomes a ripple, then disappears. The rhythm of the right hand gradually starts to fall out of step with the slow, methodical repetition in the left hand, growing more insistent and frenetic, still emerging and then receding. Eventually, the discordance takes on a life of its own, and it sounds almost as if you are listening to two very different conversations. For a time, it seems as if this strange clash of peacefulness and dispiritedness is to continue indefinitely, until suddenly, cleverly, without the listener aware of the movement, the lines are woven into consonance again. Gently, the piece descends into its final, open chord, in sonic unity once more.

Through his thoughtful, patient improvisation, Evans draws the listener into an affective encounter with the complications of peace—of finding it, staying within it, recognizing the dissonance of life around it, and yet still ultimately continuing its stately, elegant work until that dissonance is once again brought into harmoniousness. The extemporaneous nature of the piece, recorded only once with no additional takes, is drawn not from a predefined musical analogy of peace but Evans's interpretation of it through his own emotional journey in music. It is perhaps not surprising that "Peace Piece" would go on to become one of his most popular works; and yet, Evans almost never performed the piece again after that initial recording. It is almost as if Evans wanted us to know that what was communicated through that strange, transcendent moment can't ever be replicated; that improvisation, by its very nature, willingly opens itself up to the expression of luminosity through the means of the receiver, in a way that allows us to experience something beyond our capacity to control.

Music as improvisation in some ways sums up the whole of our conversation on music. Improvisation gets into the very grooves of the space between heaven and earth, between the boundaries of our limitedness and the dynamic infinitude of God's work in and through the world around us. It doesn't deny our experience of the finite world but remains open to the in-breaking of the divine life in and through our play, our music. Improvisation becomes a lively way to imagine how our finite lives and God's divine life are intertwined by the movement of the Holy Spirit, how when we are open to that motion, not caught up in our limitations but open to what God might do with us and in us and through us, we will be amazed at the beauty that can result.

The Light beyond the Music

Music, then, is a way of participating in the heavenly reality of the Father in whom all things have their source; of corresponding with the one who has bridged the space between heaven and earth for us, Christ; and through the vivifying, improvisatory movement of the Holy Spirit, of enlivening our openness to that divine reality in and through our limited selves. Music helps us experience, in a real and affective way, how the world we live in now is ever imbued with an overflowing plenitude of God's goodness that invites us to go further up and further in to that goodness.

While music is about hearing and speaking through the means of a sacramental world, the next chapter, delves into another form of communication, one not received aurally but rather visually. Image is a way of catching the rays of a heavenly light refracted through the seen world around us and receiving an image of ourselves in the aspect of the divine eyes which regard us through the form and expression of visual beauty.

COMMON SENSES

- Reflect on a personal memory that involves music. Were you listening? Performing? Were you alone? With friends or family? What makes the memory so resonant with you? What thoughts and feelings does recalling the music bring up for you? Share those thoughts and feelings with God in a time of prayer.

- Select a piece of music to give your full attention to—perhaps "Peace Piece" by Bill Evans, or "Saturn" by Sleeping at Last, or Olivier Messiaen's *Quartet for the End of Time*, or some piece of music that is meaningful to you. Note the things that distract you from this exercise—thoughts, worries, background noises, your phone. Ask God to help you lay those distractions aside. After you've finished listening, take some time to journal your thoughts and feelings.

5
DIVINE LIGHT THROUGH EARTHLY GLASS

Receiving God's Illumination
in Art and Artistry

⌇

All things are perceived in the light of charity,
and hence under the aspect of beauty: for beauty
is simply Reality seen with the eyes of love.

EVELYN UNDERHILL

In a church in Scotland where I have often sung as a choir member, there is a stained-glass window placed in a side wall, near the altar. The window can only be seen when one enters the chancel, the area where the choir sings, and thus would usually only be revealed to those who choose to come forward for Communion. However, because this church is an Anglican church, the choir stalls on either side of the aisle don't face forward toward the altar, but rather sideways, toward each other. The window is placed directly over the north choir stall, and as such, someone placed in the south choir stall can ponder it at length. This is where I have often found myself, participating as a bass in the choir.

The window is rather unique and related to the history of the church in which it is placed. It depicts the moment Christ calls Peter and Andrew to leave their fishing nets and follow Him. The window is well suited to a church that was originally founded at the end of the nineteenth century so as to serve the poorest community in town, the fishermen and their families, who made up the bulk of the local economy but who could not afford to purchase a family pew in the wealthier parish across town. The window honors by name the bishop who helped bring the church into being, a priest who indeed became not only a fisher of men but also a fisher of fishermen.

For me, the window became a way to reflect on the meaning and value of the church not only as a universal, mystical body of believers throughout time and space but also as a collection of rooted, local communities faithfully following the call of the gospel in their own cultural moment. By gazing on it during Sunday-morning services, watching as the bright light of the sun shines through it, I have often been filled with an awareness of the light of Christ burning bright in the faithful lives of all those around me, an awareness that deepens my desire to share in fellowship and communion with them.

From time to time, I have also participated in the parish's once-a-month traditional Evensong, an Anglican service of prayer at dusk. The first time I performed in an Evensong there, I remember being surprised as I looked up to the familiar window above; unlike Sunday-morning services, when the lines and hues of the fishers of men window had always been clearly articulated by the luminance of sunlight, in the dim shadows of evening, the scene had become completely incomprehensible, a mere slab of opaque glass. Without external illumination, the *telos* of the window, its end purpose, had been removed. As I pondered the window, it struck me that the inherent value of the glass, written into its very design, is only found in something external, something beyond the artistry of the image itself. The exquisite colors and contours that make up the unique image are not manifested by virtue of their own operation but instead are brought to life by light itself.

My experience with stained glass in that little Anglican parish in Scotland gave me a vision for the way imagery works its effect on us. In visual imagery—whether fine art, stained glass, or even architecture—what gives meaning and value to that visual expression is not solely in itself but rather *that in which it participates*. A thoughtfully constructed building might direct our gaze according to the proportion it provides in reference to its surroundings; a painting draws us into the narrative space of its subject matter, allowing us to transcend the canvas and enter into the scene itself, as if it were, in some sense, momentarily real; a sculpture might set off the natural light and shadow of a given space so as to more readily reveal the curves and crevices of its design. In a similar sense, for those who express the incarnate life of Christ through their own creative work, that participation becomes transposed to a spiritual level, in which the meaning of the work is made manifest by the God whose light shines through it, and who suffuses the whole world in His light.

This understanding of the visual finds its roots in the earliest practice of Christian worship and has been forcefully defended by Christians as a key means through which to know and believe in Christ, in whom are mysteriously fused both divine and human natures.

The Role of Images in Faith

In AD 787, church leaders from all over the known world at the time gathered in Nicaea, near what we know today as Istanbul, Turkey, to discuss the problem of images in Christian worship. Since the fourth-century legalization of Christianity in the Roman Empire under Emperor Constantine, holy images had been in use in prayer and for worship throughout the whole of the church; and yet, nearly as quickly as the widespread use of sacred imagery emerged, a countertrend arose to combat it: *iconoclasm*. Iconoclasts' modus operandi was found in a shocking and destructive act: the smashing of sacred depictions. From stained glass to stone mosaics, from liturgical textiles to the painted wood of icons themselves, iconoclasts destroyed any artistic depiction in spaces of worship or Christian spiritual discipline and were particularly fervent to demolish images showing any aspect of Christ or His earthly life: His mother Mary or His disciples, scenes from His earthly ministry, crucifixion, death, or resurrection. In the century prior to the Second Council of

Nicaea, as the gathering in 787 would later be named, iconoclasm had intensified, and many Christians who venerated
holy images were persecuted, even causing some to flee to the
farthest reaches of the Byzantine Empire, lest they be put to
death. Even the council itself struggled to keep order while
they debated the use of images in worship; it was delayed a
year as militant iconoclasts disbanded the gathering, causing
the Byzantine government to intervene to allow the council
to proceed. When the council finally convened, the swift
conclusion made clear that iconoclasm was not only wrong
but a radical alteration of the long tradition of artistic representation in the worship of the church, stretching back to
its earliest moments:

> We declare that we defend free from any innovations all
> the written and unwritten ecclesiastical traditions that
> have been entrusted to us. One of these is the production
> of representational art; this is quite in harmony with
> the history of the spread of the gospel, as it provides
> confirmation that the becoming man of the Word of God
> was real and not just imaginary, and as it brings us a
> similar benefit.[1]

At its core, this argument suggests that Christ Himself is
an *image*; as we've already learned from Colossians, "Christ
is the image of the invisible God."[2] In this poetic expression from Paul can be seen a powerful defense of the use of
image. Christ Himself, the one on whom humanity itself

gazed during His earthly life, an undeniable flesh-and-blood reality, was, even in that enfleshed, limited human form, the *depiction* of the *unseen* God. The eternal, ineffable God of the universe was made visible to us through Jesus Himself; in His human revelation, both natures are revealed to us. Not only is this expression in contrast to the accusations of the iconoclasts, it actually turns the accusation back around on them: To deny that Christ, or people and stories from the sacred text of Scripture, can be depicted in image, is to deny that Christ Himself was the revealed Son of God in human form. It is, in short, to deny His humanity, a heresy so profound that each of the six prior councils of the church had in some way dealt with it. Now, in this pivotal moment, the depiction of Christ through images, and holy depictions of various sorts, became not only approved as a good but as an irreplaceable defense of the two-natured Christ, the mystery at the very core of Christian faith, which the first council of Nicaea four centuries prior had fought so hard to defend. In short, Jesus is Himself an image of God, and through Jesus, we are given a template for the way in which images can open a vision of the unseen, the realm beyond our own which our eyes cannot behold directly. Though beholding an image heightens praise, it does not do so for the image itself, which would indeed be idolatry, bur rather for the sake of what is beyond it that emanates through the image and transcends it:

> Certainly this [veneration] is not the full adoration in
> accordance with our faith, which is properly paid only to

the divine nature . . . Indeed, *the honor paid to an image traverses it, reaching the model,* and he who venerates the image, venerates the person represented in that image.[3]

The image itself, which is made in reference to its subject, does not itself contain the fullness of what it depicts but rather carries the viewer through that impression toward the true person beyond it, and all that such a person represents.

One of the earliest and most arresting depictions of Jesus gives expression to this understanding of image. The Christ Pantocrator, or quite literally "Christ the Almighty," is an iconographical stylization of Jesus which depicts both His nature as the good shepherd who is near to humanity and, at the same time, His eternal kingship, through which He will judge the world at the end of time. To this end, the Pantocrator subdivides the image of Christ by depicting differing attributes of His person in His left and right side. The oldest and most famous Pantocrator, the Pantocrator at Saint Catherine's Monastery at Sinai in Egypt, remains one of the best iterations of this dual-natured image. Christ's right half, representing His nature as the loving and caring God, is depicted with soft facial features and kind eyes. His hand is held up in a two-fingered blessing, with which He sanctifies His people for Himself. Starkly contrasting this is His left half, which presents a muscular face with a downturned eyebrow, hovering over a widely opened eye staring fiercely at the viewer. In the hand of this side of the image, Christ holds the Gospel, the eternal book of the righteousness of

God. This is the Christ who comes to enact judgement on the earth, the one who did not come to abolish the law but to fulfill it in Himself.

Were the viewer to consider either half on its own, they would receive a one-sided, narrowly didactic representation of one of Christ's natures. Taken together, however, the viewer is forced to regard at the same time both the gentle kindness of a good savior and the King of heaven before whom all tremble. The Pantocrator is meant to do more than merely express a simple, streamlined truth about Jesus, but rather to help the viewer perceive the inexplicable, interwoven divine and human natures of Jesus in encounter with Jesus Himself; indeed, to contemplate the Pantocrator is to be thrust beyond easy comprehension into a confrontation with the person of Christ, in whom, beyond any human understanding, divinity and humanity are bound up in one individual. Like the window of the fishermen in my church in Scotland, the essence of the image is lit with the illumination of the one who infinitely sums up the finite theological capacity of the image; and our contemplation is not placed on the theological tenets expressed in the image but on the one beyond the image who embodies that expression, the divine logos, the Word made flesh. The image compels us to see, through its visualized aspects, the real, incarnated person beyond it.

And just as the *content* of an image can direct our gaze beyond itself toward the living subject of that image, so, too, can the color, texture, and style bring us into a deeper participation with what lies through—and beyond—the image.

Color, Time, and Memory

Since the advent of photography at the beginning of the nineteenth century, one of the great pursuits was to achieve the full colorization of captured images. Though color photography was achieved within fifty years of the first produced photographs, the widespread use of color in amateur photography would not become established until a century later. By and large, the vast collection of photographs we have from that first century and a half are in a variety of simple tones, usually a variant of monochrome (a single shade of gray), grayscale (black and white), or sepia (an alteration to grayscale). The consequence of this might affect each of us differently, depending on whether we grew up in a time before color photography, but perhaps for most of us, there is a sense that such photography is *distanced* from our current experience. The lack of color tends to affirm to us such images are *old*, that they are from the past, from a time no longer accessible to the stunning color and detail of our image-pervasive world. It distances us from the subjects of the images, such that we find it difficult to think of ourselves in the time and space of that moment. There is an unspoken wall, constructed by the stuff of our own memories, which speaks in no uncertain terms that these scenes are not from the world as we know it, our accumulation of experience; they are on the other side of an uncrossable chasm of time.

A new digital revolution in photography is turning the tide on this unsurpassable barrier. Digital colorization is providing means of both repairing images of their flaws and filling them with bright, vibrant hues that give unprecedented detail to the settings they depict. The result is often stunning: the vague two-dimensionality of the photo is shot through with a sudden depth and nuance, pressing unnoticed details forward and arresting our attention. Trees suddenly seem set into motion, as if swaying blithely in the wind; a smile catches us off guard and draw us into the laughter waiting at the edges of it; eyes no longer grainy and colorless suddenly stare at us with lively expectation, and we can't help but feel somehow those eyes contain a real, human heart hidden behind them, with a depth of meaning and value that was previously obscured from view. The past of these photos from a time before our own is made imminently real to us, and even images of cultures and places lost to the annals of history linger in our minds as if we have suddenly stumbled on a reality hidden within our own world. The barrier of time is felled with a crash, and the past of the image flows like water from a broken dam into our present.

This is the potency with which color alters our perception of the world in which we live. The vivacity of hue brings liveliness to the curves and angles of our world, such that we receive in them more than they can themselves communicate. We all know this feeling intrinsically in the changing of the seasons: when the sparse shades of winter's barren branches suddenly erupt with the budding life of spring, the promise of that new life, of the returning of warmth and happiness and sunlight, is caught up in vermillion and pink of cherry blossoms, or the bourgeoning emerald of leafy canopies above our heads. Color speaks beyond what we see to our very perception of reality itself, enlivening its angles, reorienting our sense of the passing of time, and invoking our memory, to draw us further into the ever-moving world.

The Hidden Sun

Color is especially reliant on its relationship with light to guide our focus toward a given point. Like the sun above us on a clear day, everything we see reflects the focal point of our own bright star, and the vision of the world itself ever points in return to that source. All that we know of color in our visual intake of the world—or, for that matter, of depth, contrast, angle, proportion, or any other seen aspect of it—is dependent on this light.

The most famous painting by the late-nineteenth-century painter Eugène Burnand is *The Disciples Peter and John Running to the Sepulchre on the Morning of the Resurrection.*[4] In it, the viewer is shown a vision of the two disciples—one young, beardless, and clothed in white, with a passionate longing in his features; and the other, old, gray, with haggard hair and beard, robed in dark colors, with a look of astonished hope written into the worried lines of his worn face. Their bodies are angled heavily toward the left side of the painting, as if in frantic motion. Behind them, an open landscape reveals a scene on the edges of dawn, with a scattering of purple clouds hovering behind. The color and proportion of the image is striking in itself, opening up a sense of urgency and expectation; and yet, there is an additional aspect, the source of which remains out of frame in the image, that provides the viewer with the understanding that this expectation will not be disappointed. For on the leading edge of the violet clouds behind, rich orange and gold burns out in the direction of the disciples' sprint. And in their eyes, a warm, reflective glow of what remains just beyond the left edge of the frame catalyzes the anticipation which their bodies express in their movement. It is in the use of light, and particularly the placing of the source of that light out of the frame, that the narrative gives impetus to the painting, evoking both the literal and the metaphorical dawn which the disciples seek. For the hidden sunlight plays not only as answer to the promise written in the illuminated colors of the image, but as the heightening of the desire for what the disciples themselves seek and yet remains just out of frame, the risen Christ. The use of light in Burnand's painting plays as the catalyst which invokes in our hearts the same hope implanted in the two disciples, the longing for the rising of Christ, the sun of righteousness, to burst bright and true over the shadowy landscapes of our lives.

This sense of the way light plays with color to heighten our spiritual awareness of that which we receive through our sight has a long and storied history, and one of the most potent expressions of it is in the medieval tradition of illuminating manuscripts.

Illuminated manuscripts are iterations of the words of Scripture brought into animated life by vibrant patterns, colors, textures, and depictions surrounding the words. The best way to imagine an illuminated manuscript if you have never seen one might be to think of it as stained glass on parchment; and like stained glass, it reveals the stories of the Bible in vivified visual expression. The artisan monks who brought this magnificent work to bear spared no expense in their craftsmanship: they used pigments and inks of the rarest materials, from blue Persian lapis lazuli to crimson-hued kermes from the Mediterranean Sea, from precious silver to exceedingly rare gold flake. The artisans of these illuminated manuscripts collected and expertly applied such extravagant elements toward a singular purpose: to beautify and sanctify the glorious words of sacred Scripture.

Many of the most captivating works of illumination were completed during times of great turmoil. The Book of Kells, perhaps the most known and most celebrated illuminated manuscript preserved up to our own time, was completed even in light of multiple Viking raids, and amid the death and destruction of the sacking of monasteries, with monks fleeing into the hills. The strange contrast between the industriousness of the exquisite craftsmanship that produced such brilliant and beautiful works and the impinging existential threat of war and violence which cast such communities into the dire circumstances of mere survival is stark indeed. What could possibly cause these monks to persist in such a seemingly excessive pursuit during such pressing, challenging times?

Like the discussion in chapter two about the drama of Scripture, for these monastic orders, to read the gospel was not merely to receive information but rather to engage with a living story. The text on the page was more than a mere collection of words; it was the light of God's divine truth shining out into the lives of all who read it. In a time before mass printing, when every text had to be produced by hand, the value of a single manuscript was far beyond what we could understand in our own time of literary proliferation. And these monks knew that unlike any other book in the world, the bracing words of the prophets and apostles, the enlivening poetry of the Psalms and the prose of the Gospels, each verse of Scripture was the inspired word of God, and thus was a witness to the true word, the living Logos, Christ, whose presence shone through it. Any book was rare in that time; but the words of Scripture were beyond price itself. To bring anything less than the most expressive and glorious of casts and hues to bear would be to dim the inner light imbued in the words themselves.

And just as the words of the Bible flow out into the drama of our lives, so, too, do we bear forth the spirit of emanating light expressed in illuminated manuscripts. For we are also made for illumination. Like images which reveal the goodness of their color, texture, and movement through the in-breaking of light, we were made to be bearers of a divine light, which similarly animates us.

Light Bearers

In a different part of the sanctuary in my church in St Andrews, tucked away in the corner of a high ceiling, another window provides an unexpected (and perhaps unintended) engagement with light that interacts with those who gather for worship below. Because of its placement, and because it is made up of regular clear glass rather than the stained glass of the rest of the interior, during morning services on a clear day, sunlight pours through and down into the apse below, where the congregants sit in their pews. Often, during a homily or while kneeling during the prayers of the people, I'll glance over toward the gathered congregation and see a strange, otherworldly sight: a single beam of light, pouring down into the congregation, its path articulated by the swirling mist of incense, falling on a favored individual. Often, they will have their eyes closed against the blinding brightness, which only serves to heighten the sense of the strange, heavenly calm, the sudden instance of an eternal brightness pressing out at the seams of the world in our moment of worship. A few moments later, the beam will have selected another person, and then another, moving with graceful elegance along rows of the gathered faithful, as if to reveal their inner selves, the true glory present in them, so often obscured behind the preoccupation of everyday life, but now brought to the fore in worship. As if momentarily transported to the mount of transfiguration, they burn bright with the Christ-light within them, and I find myself humbled and awed, transfixed in the gaze of a divine love. And I am reminded that even in my imperfection, even in my uncertainty and apprehension, I, too, bear that fire in me, and the loving gaze I perceive in the transfigured images of my fellow Christian brothers and sisters is on me as well, waiting to set my heart aglow.

Like stained glass which refracts sunlight into the inner world of a church sanctuary, or like sacred images which channel the eye of the beholder outward to the person who is the fullness of what the image contains, every human bears an imprint of an image, an image which, in Christ, might be set aflame with heavenly light. We who know and follow Jesus are *illuminated images*, made to reflect the divine light of Jesus to a world in need, acting as sacred depictions of God's love which might redirect longing eyes toward the fulfillment of their desires in Him.

And we are able to be such expressions of grace not only because of our witness to the light but because *we are seen by the light*. As Christ-bearing images, we receive the love of a Father who has adopted us as sons and daughters. The delight we behold in the aspect of His eyes is the love He has for us, and the joy He takes in bearing forth the life of His light through His Son in us.

To truly behold the sacredness imbued in image, to apprehend the divine light expressed within it, is not merely to *see* but to *be seen*. The transcendent joy of the visual world which we receive every day is not truly in what we do to behold but in what God does to make us light bearers. When, as Christians, we see, when we comprehend, we do it from the basis of the gift of God's self to us in and through Christ. This gift is the image placed within our very selves from the beginning, and it is the restoration of the illumination of that image once more through God's gift of Himself that amid the many who wander in darkness, we might, in the words of Philippians, "shine among them like stars in the sky as [we] hold firmly to the word of life."[5]

This notion of givenness is present in another sense faculty as well, a sense on which many great goods and profound evils rest, a sense which tips the scales in one of these directions depending on whether it is based in the economy of need and scarcity or the economy of gift. The sense I speak of is touch, mediated through human contact.

COMMON SENSES

- What images do you associate with the practice of your faith? What do you picture as you pray? As you worship? What makes those images so central for your faith life?

- Reflect on the notion that you are made in the image of God and are a bearer of God's light to the world. How does the thought affect your sense of self? Your sense of mission? Consider that the people around you are also made in the image of God— even the people you find hard to be around. How does that foundational truth affect your relationship with them?

6

TO TOUCH THE
FACE OF GOD

*Encountering God's Kindness
in Human Connection*

If we could see that Christ is the needy one . . .
and in each human figure
so shamefully thrown by our roadsides
could see Christ himself cast aside,
we would pick him up like a medal of gold
to be kissed lovingly.

OSCAR ROMERO

I can still recall the feeling of illness in my childhood. From
my youngest age, illness was nearly assured to be an annual
experience for me, from minor colds and sore throats to the
most tumultuous of stomach flus. As a child with chronically
low blood pressure given to fainting spells, as well as intensely
poor inner-ear balance, stomach illnesses were particularly
hard on me, a terror that tossed me into a squall of disorientation and fear.

Always in my memory, sickness occurred in the middle of
the night, in a time outside of time, dislodged from reason or

reality, suspended in the half light of bedside lamps turned on absently by drowsy parents. In the background, I can still catch the muffled confusion of television light, turned on to distract, to pass the endless hours of feverish half-wakefulness. Sometimes it would be an audiobook instead, and I would enter in and out of awareness of disjointed story elements and strange, unfamiliar voices. After each of these were tried and found wanting, some sort of calming instrumental music would stream into the space around me. And then, eventually, after all available distraction options were exhausted, I would be returned to the unbearable void of vainly attempted sleep.

I especially recall the feeling of illness on my skin: the obtruding mugginess of the room cocooning me and aggravating the surface of my arms, at once cold and clammy, yet burning and aching with prickling pain; the thin sheen of sweat gathering on my brow, catching the locks of my hair and matting them heavily to my forehead; the sense that every contact with a bedsheet or a couch cushion could send me into convulsions again, that the very borders which articulated the space between my interior and exterior self churned and twisted in turmoil. No amount of tossing and turning could bring the calm my body yearned for, and I would writhe myself awake a hundred times in a night.

And yet, as readily as I can recall the limbo of that pain and discomfort, I am aware of another sensation, a sensation of comfort that remains clear to me now even after many years: the gentle, comforting hand of my mother. Her cool fingers would alight on my searing back and shoulders, and she would stroke me slowly and methodically, often humming a gentle melody as she did. Her hand moved evenly and gracefully over each inch of my shoulder blades, stilling the turbulent waves of illness roiling on the surface of my skin and leaving behind a covering of calm quietude. Then, as if tilling the soil of my sickness, she would take my small, frail child's arm tenderly between her thumb and forefinger, and knead my aching muscles, massaging away the impediments and perils of my ailment until each arm was aligned with peace and calm once more. Finally, as the restfulness which had been banished began to flow over me again, I felt my mother's fingers delicately stroke my brow, wiping away the damp heat of my infirmity, and allowing the assurance of drowsiness to come over me again. My final recollections before slipping beneath consciousness were of her hand, laid in blessing on my head as if a rock holding back the tide of my fear and anguish, setting a seal of peace upon me. In that final benediction of her touch, I drifted away into the stillness of sleep.

There is something immediate, something startling in the effect of touch. Like the other senses, it brings us into contact with the world around us, makes us aware of the bounding lines of the space of our lives. And yet, even more, it does something which none of the other senses can do: It brings us into direct contact with *each other*. Touch is the sacred bond that confirms, beyond any verbal expression or perceived action, that we are regarded by the other. In touch, the participation in the other is unmediated; its expression is wordlessly given and received in a symbiotic immediacy that instills within each an instantaneous *knowledge of the other* and that we are equally *known in that knowing.* That act allows us a transformative experience of others which is unavailable by simply regarding them from a distance; and yet it equally reveals as much of ourselves as the person we apprehend through human contact. There is no question that this process can be frightening, and reasonably so. Touch is intensely powerful: Touch can lead to illness and injury and violence and even death; and yet equally in its purview are healing and consolation, affection and intimacy. To refrain from touch, to never be in contact with another, is to always be abstracted from them, set at a distance, and in turn, to always be distant from a certain knowledge of ourselves. No amount of thinking thoughts of another person, of seeing them and regarding them at a distance, can replace the knowledge that comes from contact alone. In touch is a sense of the fullness of self that is both given and received; the self can no longer be kept back when in contact with another. It must either surrender to the full givenness of whatever act of contact is initiated, whether for good or ill, or it must withdraw back into itself.

Touch is so intensely powerful that without human contact, the human body itself is adversely affected. In the 1940s, researchers began to recognize a link between maternal attention and healthy infant development. Particularly through the observations of psychoanalyst René Spitz, long-term studies revealed that even when very young children were given the highest quality of care for basic needs, if they were deprived of nurturing contact and affection, especially from their mothers, they would experience severe decline in health and mental development, stunted growth, and even in some cases, death. The phenomenon was named by Spitz as "hospitalism," referring to the detriments many infants would experience when separated from human contact even while under exemplary medical care.[1] The results were painfully obvious: Human contact is not simply a peripheral aspect of our existence but is rather a crucial, integral factor in our health and well-being.

Yet a cursory glance at contemporary culture shows how perilous touch has become. Surrounding us on all sides are the equally shocking perversions of touch, in which human contact becomes weaponized and used to harm others, whether intentionally or not. From the horrors of abuse committed by pastors and priests to the ruthlessness of chokeholds in law enforcement, from harrowing stories of assault in universities and workplaces (which are so often disregarded and ignored) to the oft hidden and yet no less insidious physical violence inflicted by family members, the illness of corrupted human touch is everywhere around us. We've attempted, rightly and justly, to find a way to respond to these injustices and evils. We have set up commissions to investigate crimes and miscarriages of the law, designed initiatives to help give family members both the means and the bravery to speak up about abusers; we have only just begun to listen to the stories of both women and men who have quietly endured the pain of another's mistreatment, and we have discussions about what consent looks like and how to listen more attentively to whether that expression is or isn't being given. These things are good and necessary, and in many instances, express the power of the gospel at work, to "comfort the brokenhearted and to proclaim that captives will be released and prisoners will be freed."[2] There is much work to be done, and many of those who are willing to stand up to these dark happenings and speak light into them are living out noble vocations, often in service of the least of these.

And yet, the mere calling out of wickedness of the abuses of human touch in our society cannot in itself recover us to the fullness of a meaningful ethic of right human contact. We have begun the needed work of exposing the deeds of darkness and bringing them into the light, yet without an understanding of what it means to engage in human contact in a virtuous way, we will ever remain in uncertain waters, always at sea and never moored in the harbor of the hopeful and loving engagement with others which we so need. Wendell Berry eloquently gives voice to this crisis:

> The public language can deal . . .with pornography, sexual hygiene, contraception, sexual harassment, rape, and so on. But it cannot talk about respect, responsibility, sexual discipline, fidelity, or the practice of love.[3]

We are met with these two contradicting truths: that human contact is a profound need woven into the well-being of our bodies and that we cannot live healthily without it;

and yet at the same time, the vast expanse of potential human contact is fraught with the most profound of dangers, pressing us back in fear. How can we even begin to think of touch as a good thing when there is so much ambiguity before us?

As always, the secret awaits us in the one who gave us our senses, and who, through His own life expressed the holy potency of touch as *the gift of self.*

The Gift of the Servant Heart

Most of us know that Jesus spoke to those around Him in parables. Each arresting and multifaceted story could evoke a multitude of human emotions, from confusion, to delight, to anger, or even remorse. Each of these stories step off of the page and into our spiritual imaginations and remain an inextricable way to understand the person of Jesus. And yet, what is often hidden from us under the surface of the Gospels is the way in which many of the stories of Jesus' own life are themselves living parables. We, like the many people around Jesus who were confused by His strange allegories for the Kingdom, are perplexed, pressed, challenged by the way that Jesus lives His life, interacts with people. His very life becomes like a metaparable to us, challenging us to enter the resonances that go beyond the page and call us into devotion.

One of the key repeated elements of Jesus' life is the way that touch plays into His interaction with others. Constantly, Jesus comes into contact with those around Him. Perhaps the most profound underlying aspect of touch in the Gospels is how often Jesus heals through touch: laying hands on the sick, touching the eyes of the blind, bringing a dead girl back to life again. We know from the disciples' own testimony in that story that countless people in the ever-present crowds around Jesus were touching Him, drawing close to Him. Even when Jesus Himself does not do the touching, those who in faith touch the hem of His robe find they have received the fullness of His healing power. In Jesus is the vision of one so deeply in submission to His Father that His whole life, body and soul, is given as a gift for others. The visceral, immediate nature of this givenness reaches out of the page and draws us into awareness of it, won't let us avoid it. It challenges us, like a parable should, to enter into the story and gain a deeper understanding of the Kingdom.

Touch is so central to Jesus' heart for the world that He spent some of what He knew to be the precious, final moments of His life focused on touch as a profound gift to His disciples: stooping down and washing their feet as an act of radical humility.

One of the earliest hymns that remains in regular use in the church is "Ubi Caritas," the antiphon used for Maundy Thursday in Holy Week. The title is drawn from the first line of the hymn, which translated, says: "Where charity and love are, God is there." The hymn is in itself a beautiful reflection on the way self-giving love reveals God to us, draws us into communion with each other, and makes us ready to behold the God who is himself love:

Where charity and love are, God is there.

Christ's love has gathered us into one.

Let us rejoice and be pleased in Him.

Let us fear, and let us love the living God.

And may we love each other with a sincere heart.[4]

Maundy is an adaptation of the Latin word *mandatum*, commonly translated as "commandment." It is drawn from John 13:34, in which Jesus says to his disciples, "A new command I give you: Love one another. As I have loved you, so you must love one another."[5] Jesus said these words to his disciples right after he knelt down and washed each disciple's feet. His commandment—His mandate of love—emerged from the gravity of this act. For first-century Judea, where footwear did not reflect the advances of our own age and feet took on the filth of days of trudging in grime and grit, the act of foot-washing was one of abasement. Washing someone's feet would have been considered an offensive act for someone of any social standing. For the disciples, the cost of Jesus' self-effacing gift of touch would have been immediately obvious; it testified to the radical, sacrificial love Jesus mandated to them, and to us.

In our own time, Maundy Thursday liturgy recalls this moment in a reenactment of foot-washing, usually performed by the pastors, priests, or bishops leading the service, on members of the congregation. Though the radical nature of foot-washing may be more obscured in our own time, it remains startling to see our spiritual leaders—people for whom we reserve high respect—kneel down and tenderly clean soiled feet in their hands. Sung in the background of this liturgy, "Ubi Caritas" provides the bigger picture: It is precisely through such humble acts of self-impoverishment that the glories of heaven are opened and we are made one with God:

> Where charity and love are, God is there.
> And may we with the saints also,
> See Thy face in glory, O Christ our God:
> The joy that is immense and good,
> Unto the ages through infinite ages. Amen.[6]

In washing the feet of His disciples, Jesus revealed human touch as a manifest expression of the ability we have to give ourselves for the sake of others, to lose our lives so as to find them again in those around us. We are called to wash the feet of those around us, to reach out and come into contact with others in self-giving, to "love each other with a sincere heart," so that we may "see Thy face in glory, O Christ our God."

To touch another, in the economy of Christlike activity, is never to demand or require but rather to give, to offer freely, to empty ourselves in humility so as to be given to those around us, and in turn, to receive the gift of them. True community, and communion, only comes through this willingness to let go of our desires and instead seek the good of those around us. We don't need parables to hear it in Jesus' words throughout the Gospels, given to us plainly and directly:

Whoever wants to be first must take last place and be the servant of everyone else.[7]

Many who are the greatest now will be least important then, and those who seem least important now will be the greatest then.[8]

There is no greater love than to lay down one's life for one's friends.[9]

The taking up of the basin and the towel through human touch can be seen in any relationship: It can be seen in the embracing of a person scorned by others or when someone silently holds the hand of a grieving friend; it can be seen in the attentive affection of a parent who refuses to be embarrassed by an upset child and holds them close instead; it can be seen in the love of an adult child who has become the caregiver for their elderly parent; and when people lock arms with the oppressed to protest violence or oppression or racism, it is there too. There is no limit to the way that touch, given as gift, reveals the beauty of God's lifegiving power, drawing people together in communion and community.

The Moment of Communion

Right in the midst of a prestigious academic career in France, Henri Nouwen walked away to live quietly and simply among the developmentally disabled in Ontario. After seeing the halls of power up close in places like Yale and Harvard, Nouwen believed that contemporary culture had an upside-down view of what constitutes success and value, and that to recover a life of meaning, the answer is to let go of the desire to be great—and, by turns, the fear of rejection that paralyzes us:

> The world tells you many lies about who you are, and you simply have to be realistic enough to remind yourself of this. Every time you feel hurt, offended, or rejected, you have to dare to say to yourself: "These feelings, strong as they may be, are not telling me the truth about myself. The truth, even though I cannot feel it right now, is that I am the chosen child of God, precious in God's eyes, called the Beloved from all eternity, and held safe in an everlasting embrace."[10]

Nouwen suggests that the effect of the letting go of self-importance is not merely for ourselves but so that in seeing ourselves in the light of God's love, we are made aware of the intrinsic glory planted in each person around us, a glory that is available to us no matter the worth of that person in the world's eyes. In that space of openness, God draws all people to Himself in belonging:

> Instead of making us feel that we are better, more precious or valuable than others, our awareness of being chosen opens our eyes to the chosenness of others . . . Once we deeply trust that we ourselves are precious in God's eyes,

we are able to recognize the preciousness of others and their unique places in God's heart.[11]

In the end, this freedom shows us that by letting go of our desires to be great in the world and instead living in the love of God's gift of Himself to us, we are able to give ourselves as a gift to others and so receive our desires back in full: "Our greatest fulfillment lies in becoming bread for the world. That is the most intimate expression of our deepest desire to give ourselves to each other."[12] To give and receive in such radical freedom is to be free from the prison of self-worth, liberated into the realization of our most profound longings planted in our hearts by the God who has given Himself for us.

Perhaps one of the more visible expressions of this mutual self-giving is in the unique and sacred form of touch designed exclusively for marriage, sex, and what it naturally makes possible, new life. In sexuality as it is meant to be, emulating the servant heart of Christ, one is invited to give the fullness of themselves, and to receive the fullness of someone else in return, not holding anything back but rather letting their selves be fully given to the other and allowing the other to take their place in return. It is in this mutual self-giving between a man and a woman that something miraculous happens: Rather than a mere exchange of places, in which the two remain unto themselves, instead, both are resurrected into a new, singular whole. Sex is the sacramental action that expresses the irreversible and mystical fusion of two people who give the gift of themselves to the other and, as a result, are inextricably raised up in communion with each other. This is why for the Christian, sexuality must be in the context of marriage. The glory of sex is not meant to be found in the individual experience of each person but rather in the joy that comes from participation in and with each other. A marriage partner is not some*thing* to be objectified for pleasure, but some*one* of infinite worth to be honored in intimacy. The symbiosis of gift in sex means that to receive the full and complete gift of the other requires the full and complete gift of one's self in return.

The sign of that new communion is the potential for new human life. Whether new life results from sex or not, children are inextricably interwoven with Christian sexuality, because a child becomes a living and beloved expression of gift in marriage. It mirrors the way in which we received new life through God's incarnation, God's self-giving of Himself, through Christ being enfleshed in our human form. From incarnational self-giving, new life begins. The beauty of a new life must remain a crucial potential of Christian eros, for sexuality, like all human contact in Christian practice, is imbued with the capacity to sacramentally testify that, by giving touch as a gift, faith, hope, and charity are born anew in the world.

We need these examples of courage in giving our contact as gift, because in marriage and friendship, in parenthood and childhood, in every sort of relationship, to give and receive means to accept not only the joy inherent in that gift but the wounds that come with it as well. It is to take on their sufferings, and in so doing, receive the suffering Savior through them.

To Share in the Wounds of Another

Caravaggio, a painter during the Italian Baroque period, used light and shadow to dramatic effect in his paintings through his self-developed style, entitled *chiaroscuro*. Later known as *tenebrism*, from the Latin word *tenebrae*, meaning "darkness," chiaroscuro allowed Caravaggio to set the subjects of his paintings against a black backdrop and use light to illuminate various aspects of their bodies. As such, the contours of human expression in Caravaggio's subjects, their posture and gesture and facial variance, which would otherwise blend into the background, are illumined and crystalized into deeper meaning.

In Caravaggio's painting *The Incredulity of Saint Thomas*,[13] Thomas leans forward intently toward a resurrected Jesus, who has pulled back His cloak to reveal an open wound on His chest. Jesus' hand confidently guides Thomas's finger into the wound, where it pushes up against the incised skin of the gash. Jesus' face itself is obscured in shadow, and instead, it is His breast, and His hand guiding Thomas's hand to the wound on His right side, that is illuminated, revealing in gritty detail the shocking spiritedness with which Jesus thrusts Thomas's finger into the wound.

The light falls on Thomas's brow, too, but it is caught in surprised wrinkles, luminance interrupted by intermittent lines of shadow. It is as if the intense contact with Christ's flesh has lit the fire of awareness of Jesus within him; and yet at the same time, the knowledge of that contact draws Thomas into participation in the suffering encased in the contours of the wound on Christ's side, an engagement shown to us through the dark lines of sadness etched into the light falling on his brow. In seemingly unconscious reaction, Thomas's left hand clutches at his own side, as if he has somehow received a reiteration of Christ's pain in his own body.

The scene is visceral and unnerving, pushing us to recognize, perhaps, the way Thomas's encounter with Jesus' body speaks to us about contact. We focus so readily on Thomas's stubborn desire to encounter Jesus in the flesh as a sign of doubt. But what if the contact with Christ's wounds reveals, through no intention of Thomas, a holy truth about knowing Jesus? Whether intentionally or not, Thomas's insistence on touching the wounds of Christ affirms Jesus as truly human and expresses to us that to truly believe in Christ is to not be satisfied with the mere notion of the other but rather to insist on the human contact which honors the divine image in each human. In that contact, Thomas becomes more deeply aware of himself, a human engaged so deeply in communion with Jesus through the power of touch that the suffering he encounters in the wound of Christ resounds in his own embodied experience. More than simply a rebuffing of doubt, Caravaggio's painting opens us up to a potentially crucial understanding of participation in Jesus: To come into contact with another person's wounds is to commune with Christ; for when we let ourselves come into contact with them, we, like Thomas, receive the sufferings of Christ manifested in that person. To hold those around us at a distance and merely acknowledge their lives and sorrows at arm's length is to hold Jesus Himself at a distance.

Mother Teresa, the twentieth-century Albanian nun who cared for the sick and dying in the slums of Calcutta, was particularly focused on the illness of leprosy. Because of fear that the disfiguring disease was highly contagious, many who contracted leprosy were immediately cast out by their families, to die alone and uncared for. Mother Teresa spent her life surrounded by her fellow sisters in the Missionaries of Charity, the religious order she founded in 1950, caring for the sick and tending to the dying. Even while the whole of society around them recoiled from the leprous in fear, Mother Teresa drew near to them in close human contact: bathing them, tending to their wounds, comforting them in illness, and holding them as they approached death. Mother Teresa understood the love of Christ that can only be given and received in the touch of another and saw how distorted contemporary life is in this regard, how far it has distanced us from this kind of love:

> The greatest disease in the West today is not [tuberculosis]
> or leprosy; it is being unwanted, unloved, and uncared for.
> We can cure physical diseases with medicine, but the only

cure for loneliness, despair, and hopelessness is love. There are many in the world who are dying for a piece of bread but there are many more dying for a little love.[14]

And how ought we express this love? Through the grace of human contact, says Mother Teresa:

Let us touch the dying, the poor, the lonely and the unwanted according to the graces we have received and let us not be ashamed or slow to do the humble work.[15]

When we allow ourselves to encounter the suffering in others, we express the incarnate love of Jesus in a way that no mere statement of love could ever achieve. If Augustine is right, that a sacrament is an outward sign of an inward grace, then in allowing ourselves to come into contact with the sufferings of others, we become embodied sacraments which imbue the grace of Christ through our own bodies.

Sacramental Witness

And we don't achieve this sacramental witness through any means in ourselves. Instead, we do it in emulation of our Master, the one who showed us through His life what the gift of human contact looks like, how healing and life are inextricably wrapped up into it. The gift that Jesus gave through His life, death, and resurrection is not only salvation or the restoration of our relationship with God, but rather the gift of Himself, a gift we are recalled to anew each time we participate in the Lord's Supper. We already witnessed how Jesus allowed His life to be given in close, healing contact with others, to make His body a conduit of God's restoration that bestowed healing; but the completion of the healing ministry of Jesus doesn't end after the last of His earthly miracles. It is instead made manifest in the final and utter giving of His body for the world, in suffering and death on the cross. In 1 Corinthians, Paul reminds us to ever recall Christ's words, to keep them close at hand: "This is my body, which is given for you. Do this in remembrance of me."[16] Whenever we participate in the Communion table, whether we believe that participation to be only a memorial or something more, we are confronted with the terrible and glorious beauty of Christ's body given for us, and as we receive the bread and the wine into our bodies, we are provoked into the awareness of what it means to give our bodies, through human contact, as complete gift, just as Jesus gave His for us. To return to the table is to accept this call, this vocation, and to make it manifest in our lives anew every day.

How can we move toward this openness? How can we train ourselves to be attentive to others, to live and act as if our lives and our actions and our sensory engagements are to be given as gift? There is an ancient way, a rhythm given to us for fallow seasons, that helps us hone our senses and make them more alert to such a Christ-imbued life. Fasting makes a way for us to clean the windows of our souls.

COMMON SENSES

- Reflect on some memory of being shown love or compassion through touch. Who was involved? What led to the encounter? What sensations do you remember? What makes it such a resonant memory for you?

- Many people have experiences of touch that are painful, even violent. If memories of experiences like that are resurfacing for you, bring them before God in prayer. Ask Him to overwhelm the sense of hurt with His provision of love. Consider sharing your story with someone trustworthy who can help you process that experience, perhaps a counselor or other mental health professional.

- Who in your life would be blessed by a compassionate, loving, serving touch from you? Plan to extend this act of kindness to that person.

7
THE HOLY ART OF WINDOW WASHING

Seeking God's Renewal in Fallow Seasons

⌒

It is impossible to enter into the mystery of God
without entering into the solitude and silence of
our interior desert.

ROBERT CARDINAL SARAH

No Wi-Fi.

When I first got the email from my friend inviting me to
a writing retreat in the Scottish Highlands, I confess that this
line, hidden away amid a list of all the delightful and exciting
features of the weekend, was the one that stood out. I knew,
beyond a shadow of a doubt, that I was fast approaching that
point of stagnation that comes over all writers, when they've
parked themselves in the same surroundings for just a bit too
long. I knew that such a weekend would be just the remedy
to return my muse to me and set me back to rights.

But *no Wi-Fi?*

In the car on the way up the farm where we would be

staying, the nagging concern of being disconnected for several days straight mixed together with a heightened impulse to check my phone every few minutes, an ingrained habit only intensified by my impending digital blackout. Finally, out of the coastal cities of Dundee and Aberdeen and well into the foothills of the Cairngorms, the collection of peaks that make up the beginning of the Highlands, the dreaded message appeared on my screen:

No service.

I sighed, absently glancing out the window. Bright, golden sheaves of wintery barley whisked by in a blur, set into a rolling landscape of emerald green, shimmering even in February's dormant chill. Even further beyond, sloping hills gave way to mountains, snowcapped and jutting at bold angles against a pastel sky. Flocks of birds burst like scatter shot upward from nowhere, gathering into murmurations which solidified and disintegrated a dozen times in the blink of an eye. Dazzled, I let myself be carried away for a time, lulled by the rambling of the car along the narrow, curving carriage road. Then, as if on cue, my hand slipped down unconsciously and pulled my phone out of my pocket again. Obediently, my eyes followed suit, turning to my digital lifeline with no intended plan except to be distracted and diverted. I immediately realized the futility of the action, given that we were now even further from service than we had been before; and yet, in addition to that realization, another which had long lain asleep under the surface of my mind suddenly sprung to life: the awareness of the utter sterility and banality of the image before me compared to the visual feast I had just beheld. Surprised and chastened by the sentiment, I put the phone back in my pocket and returned my eyes to the scene beyond.

Later (and after a half-dozen additional subconscious glances at my phone), we arrived at our destination. The old farmhouse was perched high on a hill, overlooking a far-stretching valley, beyond which arose the arresting figure of Ben Rinnes, the highest peak in the area. As we unpacked our things into a disordered pile in the entry hallway, we opened curtains covering the long vista window which ran the length of the kitchen and dining room, looking toward the valley. Even though it was only midafternoon, in true Scottish fashion, the winter sun had begun to set early, and left only a ridgeline of gleaming firelight along the top of the lonely mountain. The sky-flames of vermillion melted into a deep indigo, and above that, the first gentle appearance of starlight peered down. For a moment, we were all silent in captivated wonder, until our host piped up excitedly, "Let's go for a walk before it gets too dark!" Had I been at home, looking at a glorious sunset out my window, perhaps I would have marveled for a moment before being called back to Netflix or Facebook or missed emails, a million little slices against my focused attention. But here, the enamor of what lay before me was unmediated. It called me, pressed me, even admonished me. I suddenly felt a strange shame come over me, that I would ever think to turn down such an opportunity. For the second time that day, I found myself bewildered by an inner voice speaking to me, an inner voice long muffled but suddenly brought into bright clarity.

Later that night, tucked into the warmth of the farmhouse and gathered with friends, we talked and laughed and shared about our lives and our hopes. We ate a homemade meal around a table and toasted each other in cheerful fellowship. Afterward we took up banjo and ukulele and laughed as we strummed out folk tunes and favorite songs. Finally, as we said our goodnights and headed to our various rooms, I felt the inner voice begin to speak to me, with words long buried under the dusty heap of my busyness and distraction: *The world is ever waiting for you only to look up and see it.*

The following days of the trip are equally vibrant in my memory. Each recollection comes to me with startling clarity even now: The way the light crossed along and through pine boughs, or the mossy green of the damp carpet covering the northern sides of trees; the smiles of friends and the tranquility of their camaraderie; the tantalizing taste of freshly baked bread served straight out of the oven; the sense of real, abiding rest, of fully entering into quietude around me, not interrupted by notification alerts or phone calls or text messages; the breath of God's spirit on the wind, flowing past my face, and the light of His countenance in the sun warming me as I lay in the heather on the hill above the farm.

After three days which seemed to contain the fullness of a year's worth of goodness, it was time to return to our regular lives in St Andrews, to pick up our responsibilities once more and enter the fray again. And yet, as we retraced our outward journey along narrow roads through the mountains, my eyes were alert and aware. In the misty shroud that followed us all the way home, I felt, in my innermost self, that there was more in each blade of dew-strewn grass, each tree and hill and silvery moor, pressing out, seeking something within me; and in my heart, that inner self, the one whose voice had finally made itself heard over the weekend, leapt up in ardent answer to that call. Whereas it had languished behind the grime and grub of the frenetic distraction of my life, now, the window of my soul had been cleaned, cleared. The image of the divine heart pressing out through the world around me was as evident as daylight.

To Brighten the Stars

More than anything else I have expressed to you in this book, I hope you have gathered that we are created to experience God through our senses, and in that encounter, to come to know Him better and grow in love. And yet, even our senses themselves can become overloaded; the windows of our souls become covered in grime, and without realizing it as it happens, we lose our grasp of the vision of the good, the true, and the beautiful. Whether through the negative habits of sin, or perhaps even more often through the glut of filling our lives with too much busyness, too many experiences, stretching ourselves thin among the endless demands of our lives, even when those demands are worthy and good, we find that the world becomes separated from us, difficult to access. We find that we are distanced from the very world with which our senses are made to come into contact.

It is into this distancing that the gift of fasting becomes a way forward for us, a way of return to that contact with the holy through our senses. Fasting is the ancient practice of temporarily stripping away the things in our lives that demand our attention and affection for the sake of prayer and reflection. Perhaps the most common spiritual discipline, it is enshrined in the rhythms of the liturgical church year no less than twice: during the seasons of Advent, which leads up to Christmas, and Lent, which leads up to Easter. It is both one of the oldest spiritual disciplines in the church and one of the most misunderstood. It is easy to understand why: By taking away food, drink, and other good things that become pathways for our senses, how can we think of fasting as anything less than a disdain of the senses, a belief that somehow, at heart, they are wrong and will mislead us? It could almost seem as if, afraid that we will become too indulgent, the church institutes these seasons to diminish the senses, to make sure we don't give them too much precedence.

The tradition of fasting in Christian practice tells a very different story. Far from being a rejection of the senses, fasting intrinsically recognizes the *power* of the senses in our lives and how they shape us and form our experience of reality. The various sensory points of contact with the world, whether good or evil, do not simply engage our senses. They engage our *hearts through our senses*. Our senses are channels, conduits of God's revelation of Himself in the created world, and reveal to our hearts what our minds alone cannot comprehend or make sense of. Our senses are our only doorway to the world as it is given to us through the tangible and the experienced. Not only do our senses afford us an encounter with God through the tangible aspects of the world around us, as we have discussed in so many different ways in this book so far; even the knowledge and understanding of who God is, and who Jesus is as a revelation of that God, are received through our senses. It is with our ears that we hear the good news of the gospel preached, and our eyes that we read the words of Scripture. We receive testimony of the spirit of Jesus living in others through observation of their actions, the way they treat others and the world around them. Without our senses, we would be helpless to know God at all. The disposition of our senses, their health and vitality at any given point in our lives, is of the utmost importance because our ability to receive God's goodness depends on their continued conveyance of that goodness.

Fasting gives high honor to the way in which the senses direct our desires: It expresses the peril of a wrongly trained sense to lead us into deeply harmful and broken practices, and it equally acknowledges the power of the redeemed senses to be used to heighten one's awareness of God and cultivate their desires to participate in His life. To fast is not to *reject* the senses, but to *reform* them, to *reorient* them and allow them to be *retrained*. It is, paradoxically, a radical *embrace* of the senses, cleaning away the grimy film that gathers on the windows of our hearts, so that we can see again with a renewed inner eye and recognize the luminance shining out of all things once more.

Orthodox theologian and musician Peter Bouteneff beautifully encapsulates this sensibility while discussing the most important fasting season in the Orthodox Church calendar, the six weeks leading up to Holy Week and Easter:

> Great Lent provides a period of vigilance that will rightly prepare for the genuine and enduring joy of redemption. *It is a chosen darkening of the night in order to brighten our perception of the stars.* It is no exaggeration to say that nearly every spiritual discipline, Eastern and Western, promotes similar kinds of renunciation *in order to redirect and sharpen the senses.*[1]

Bouteneff's elegant reference to stars captures the way in which refraining from sensory engagement heightens our awareness of the one in whom "was life, and that life was the light of all mankind."[2] Both of the regular seasons of fasting in the church express this: In Advent, fasting makes us more able to enter expectation for the dawn of Christ into the world at Christmas, just as Zechariah says in Luke, "Because of God's tender mercy, the morning light from heaven is about to break upon us, to give light to those who sit in darkness and in the shadow of death";[3] and in Lent, it makes us more able to enter the darkness of that shadow, awaiting, like the disciples, the return of Christ, who destroys night forever in the morning light of His resurrection at Easter:

"Weeping may last through the night, but joy comes with the morning."[4]

In this darkening of our senses that brightens the star of Christ, as Bouteneff suggests, we become aware of another resonance of fasting, one that doesn't imply the mere removal of sensory aspects but one which brings us—through denial, through the loss of something meaningful and good in our lives—into a profound sensory experience that heightens our desire for Jesus.

The Hidden, Manifested Jesus

Many of us have likely sung the hymn "O Sacred Head, Now Wounded," but perhaps what is less known is that this classic work expressing the sorrow of Christ's crucifixion is extracted from Johann Sebastian Bach's much larger masterpiece, the *St. Matthew Passion*. In his passion setting, Bach wanted to invoke the sense of the sorrow of the crucifixion and help the listener enter into that sorrow so as to more deeply understand and embrace the suffering of the cross. Bach uses his musical composition to engage with the theology of the hidden God, the notion that God becomes more present to us even as He seems to be hidden from view. To that end, Bach uses an ever-expanding structure in each movement to pull the listener not only into Christ's passion on the cross but into a *passion for* Christ, to love Him and desire Him more deeply, even as He disappears from view in His death and entry into the grave.

The story is first set in Scripture itself, being sung through *recitatives*, or non-metric recitations, in this case of verses extracted from the biblical story. These narrations of Scripture are given straightforwardly, with little fanfare or compositional adornment; sometimes the recitations are interspersed with choruses which, in a form typical at the time for passion settings, act as the voice of various characters or of collections of characters voiced in the biblical text. These recitatives and choruses make up the basic narrative aspects of the Crucifixion story, the story which many of us know by rote.

Beyond this, however, additional solos and choral elements articulate the story within the story, the emotions of those watching the events unfold before them. In these additional moments, the music is expressive, emotive, full of ardor and drama, at times glorious and soaring, and other times plaintive and mournful. The extrabiblical, poetic text sung in these instances are not narrative but rather reflective, as if a view into the interior response of those watching the scene firsthand. These moments turn the story toward us, so instead of mere observers, we become participants receiving a real and visceral human reaction to Christ's suffering. In this way, we are pushed beyond receiving the biblical account as if a neutral stating of facts and instead enter the passion, grief, and glory hidden behind the text itself, in the redemptive drama at hand.

The final duet and chorus of the whole passion setting reveals this in full. Rather than anticipating the Resurrection, the work ends in an ambiguous space. The penultimate recitative relates the final verses of Matthew 27: "Pilate replied, 'Take guards and secure it the best you can.' So they sealed the tomb and posted guards to protect it."[5] Into the harsh finality of that text, a tender, hushed antiphonal duet between each of the soloists and the chorus opens up. Each soloist in turn expresses the way in which Christ, in His work on the cross, has completed the work of salvation. To each statement of a soloist, the chorus responds with the refrain, "My Jesus, my Jesus, good night!":

Tenor: The trouble which our sins caused him is over.
Chorus: My Jesus, my Jesus, good night!
Countertenor: Oh blessed bones, see how I mourn you with penitence and regret that my fall brought you to such distress.
Chorus: My Jesus, my Jesus, good night!
Soprano: A thousand lifelong thanks for your suffering that you so highly value the salvation of my soul.
Chorus: My Jesus, my Jesus, good night![6]

As the soloists make their statements and the chorus responds with the refrain, the music morphs; what begins in a pastoral major key becomes increasingly dissonant. By the end of the back-and-forth between soloists and chorus, the music has landed on a troubled minor tonality. This gives way to the final chorus, which expresses the way in which, even while Jesus is literally hidden away from view beyond a barrier of stone, the listener is invited to draw near to Christ, to let the innermost parts of their heart discover the hidden Christ there:

> We sit down in tears and call to you in the grave: rest
> in peace, peacefully rest, rest in peace, peacefully rest!
> Rest your exhausted limbs! Rest in peace! Your grave and
> tombstone will be a comfortable pillow and a resting place
> for the soul and for the fearful mind. Filled with pleasure,
> the eyes can sleep there. We sit down in tears and call
> to you in the grave. Rest in peace, peacefully rest, rest in
> peace, peacefully rest![7]

The music ebbs and flows in an emotive, minor key reflection, interspersing solos with full choral textures. Though the text is deferential and seemingly caught up in the surrender to the grave, the form used by Bach in this final section is a sarabande, a stately dance form. It is as if, even as the text hides Christ away in the darkness of the tomb, the music challenges this finality, provoking our hearts into a dynamic participation in contrast with the words themselves. Perhaps, in this, Bach's intention for the whole piece becomes clear: By drawing the listener into the emotive aspects of the story, in which, to the observer, Jesus is slowly hidden from view, the passion for the presence of Christ becomes profoundly more inculcated in our hearts, and we are called into a deeper devotion to His presence in our lives. It is through absence that God's presence becomes clearer and more vital to us.

This truth perhaps becomes most expressed through Holy Saturday, the final day of Lent. It is a strange interim time, between the horror of the Crucifixion on Good Friday and the joy of the Resurrection on Easter Sunday. As the final day of Lenten fasting, Holy Saturday in some ways sums up the full extent of why fasting, the purposeful removal of a sensory engagement which is valuable in our lives, is so necessary, so intrinsic to the season in which the church reflects on Jesus's passion. In his work written in tandem with the art of William Congdon, Joseph Ratzinger, the theologian and Catholic priest who would later become Pope Benedict XVI, wrote a moving reflection on the emptiness of Holy Saturday:

> On Good Friday we could at least look at the pierced one. But Holy Saturday is empty, the heavy stone of the new tomb covers over the deceased, everything is over, faith seems definitively unmasked as wishful thinking.[8]

Just as fasting strips away the sensory engagement with the world itself and distances us from our senses, so Holy Saturday becomes a way to practice an awareness of the despair of a world were it not for the liberating love of God:

> We needed the darkness of God, the silence of God, in order to experience the chasm of his greatness and the abyss of our nothingness, which would become manifest if he were not.[9]

Somehow, in the midst of this absence, we are made intensely and manifestly aware of the presence of Christ with us in our most profound moments of suffering:

> No one can imagine what the words 'descended into hell' mean in the end. But when we ourselves approach the hour of our final solitude, we will be permitted to grasp something of this dark mystery. . . . We begin to offer thanks for the light that already comes to us from this darkness.[10]

Just like in Bach's *St. Matthew Passion*, in our time of waiting on Holy Saturday, the hiddenness of Jesus, His seeming absence, becomes the thing which makes us most aware of our need for Him, of the meaning of His coming into the world and drawing us back into communion with the Father through Jesus Himself.

Fasting encapsulates this truth and teaches it to our senses: Through the absence of sensory engagement in the world, we are brought into an awareness of our need for Christ, and a profound desire for Him to manifest Himself in us. By removing our senses from their habituated norms of engagement with God for a time, fasting mysteriously heightens our desire for Christ to be real to us again, reordering our senses away from wrongful desires and back toward the profound awareness of His presence breaking through every inch of the world.

In fact, this notion is so woven into the heart of fasting that many theologians throughout the history of the church have sought to reevaluate silence and darkness not as an evil but as a good that provides us a capacity to experience God not available through our thought or sensory capacities. We have already spoken of this theological tradition, in the introduction. It is the *apophatic* way of theology, the way of denial as a means of comprehending the incomprehensible God. It is the *via negativa*, the way of negation.

The Shimmering Darkness

In his mystical treatise *The Soul's Journey into God*, medieval theologian Bonaventure reflects on steps of contemplation that lead to meaningful participation in God's presence. He takes the reader through a consideration of various aspects of prayer and meditation. He begins with the reception of God's life in the world through the senses; considers the inward beauty of the image of God within each of us; moves from that inner illumination upward toward consideration of the Trinity; and finally ends by subverting the path of contemplation he has set out. For Bonaventure, the final step in the soul's journey into God is to *let go*.

He suggests that whether it be our senses, the means through which God is revealed to us in the world, or our intellect, our capacity to understand and make sense of that world, our own faculties can only take us so far. Somehow, it is in the silence, in our willingness to admit our limitation and wait for God patiently and without demanding knowledge or understanding, that something new is born. God

Himself incarnates into the silences of our unknowing. This darkness, for Bonaventure, is where grace is received in the most manifest way; for in that darkness, in which we have given up our capacity to understand, we are most able to receive the real gift of faith:

> Ask grace, not learning; desire, not intellect; the groaning
> of prayer and not diligent reading; the Bridegroom, not the
> academic teacher; God, not a human being; darkness, not
> clarity; not light, but the fire that inflames one totally and
> carries one into God through spiritual fervor and with the
> most burning affections.[11]

In this understanding, the Cross becomes, for Bonaventure, not a sign of evil but rather of the virtue of the *via negativa*. By embracing the emptiness represented by Christ's cruci-fixion, a way is opened to us, a way which is closed to us if we refuse to let go of understanding. For Bonaventure, the Cross becomes the mystical sign through which our desire to comprehend gives way to the infinitely better experience, to commune with God, who is beyond imagination:

> Let us die, then, and enter into this darkness. Let us silence
> all our cares, desires, and images in the imagination. Let us
> pass over with the crucified Christ from this world to the
> Father, so that when the Father has been shown to us, we
> may say with Philip: It is enough for us. Let us hear with
> Paul: My grace is sufficient for you; and let us exult with

David, saying: My flesh and my heart waste away; you
are the God of my heart, and the God that is my portion
forever.[12]

For Bonaventure, the path to the fulfillment of our deepest spiritual longings is to let go of our understanding and
receive from the eternal wellspring of God's life. The path to
fullness is to dwell in the mysterious silence of God.

The contemporary Estonian composer Arvo Pärt has often
been immersed in the waters of silence. While he began his
career producing expressive, avant garde works in keeping
with other composers of the latter half of the twentieth century, only a few years into his work, he suddenly stopped writing for eight years. It is debated why it is that Pärt refrained
from producing significant new compositions during that
period. Some suggest it is because of Soviet oppression staying
his hand from the concepts he longed to express; others think
that perhaps he entered into a long dry spell, having reached a
creative wall with contemporary concert music. In any event,
when Pärt did finally begin composing again in 1976, his
musical style had radically changed, and that alteration would
prove enormously consequential for the shape of both concert
and sacred music in the last years of the twentieth century. In
short, Pärt began to compose in, through, and with silence,
by means of his own new style, *tintinnabuli*.

In this unique method, Pärt uses the barest of elements
to make up his music, only two melodic forms: one line
which repeats tonal harmonies in either arpeggios or repeated

notes of a given chord; and one line which moves in stepwise motion, gradually moving upward or downward, each note given an unusually long duration. Using only these two elements, Pärt creates open musical soundscapes which develop very slowly and often center around brief musical gestures which fade into silence and only occasionally emerge out of it again. Pärt explains his style in his own words:

> Tintinnabulation is an area I sometimes wander into when I am searching for answers . . . Here I am alone with silence. I have discovered that it is enough when a single note is beautifully played. This one note, or a silent beat, or a moment of silence, comforts me.[13]

Western music is built around the idea of theme and variation: The way to express an idea in music is to give it thematic nature, and then to develop that theme over time and use it to guide the narrative forward. Yet rather than presuming that more expression in art leads to more understanding, Pärt subverts this assumed convention, willingly restraining from strong statements and themes. The thinner and sparer Pärt's music is, the more each in-breaking note or harmony takes on meaning for the listener. It is as if Pärt wants us as the recipients of his music to keep vigil with him, to quiet ourselves and make ourselves one with the sense of emptiness in the void of silence. And when music is spoken into that void, we are able to receive, in a way that would otherwise be inaccessible to us, presence and accompaniment in that music. Into the silence of Pärt's music, we are accompanied by divine presence.

In his book on Pärt's musical theology, Bouteneff notes that a strange trend has been noticed in people who listen to Pärt's music: "People in situations of pain, people on their journey toward death, often find a curiously *empathetic* quality in Pärt's work: they feel that the music is suffering with them."[14] Noting both anecdotal and widely published accounts, Bouteneff posits that "the particular relationship between this music and those who are in acute states of suffering or in the process of dying is observed with increasing frequency."[15] Somehow, the sonic spaciousness in Pärt's works, which might otherwise seem detached and otherworldly, make space for the participation in God's presence that may not be available in a fuller, busier sound. Bouteneff explains: "The mystery is that it does not stop at sadness: embedded within it, inextricably woven into it, is a voice of genuine hope."[16]

In the very heart of suffering, in the impending silence of death, in the most inexplicable moments, paradoxically, the feeling of relief, or of hope, comes not through seeking to fill the void but rather by embracing the unknown emptiness and finding within it the God who loves us and meets us in that darkness.

From Mourning to Morning

This is indeed at the very heart of fasting: not a denial for denial's sake, not a self-hatred or mistrust of the senses, but instead a turning that makes the encounter with the living Christ—who has entered into our world and become part of our lives, our joys and our sufferings alike—more manifest.

Thankfully, the discipline of fasting is not the last word on the senses or on participation in Jesus through the world around us. Like the waters of Baptism that submerge us prior to our entry into the Kingdom, like the veil of death that precedes resurrection, like the entirety of our finite earthly lives that come before our entry into eternity, fasting is only the prelude. We might recall the psalmist's words at the beginning of this chapter and hear them anew: "Weeping may last through the night, but joy comes with the morning."[17]

For after the fast comes the feast.

COMMON SENSES

- Reflect back on a time you experienced the "mysterious silence of God." What sustained you through it? Assuming that time of God's silence came to an end, how have you made sense of it as you've continued to practice your faith?

- Consider an experiment in fasting—from food (giving consideration to any health concerns), from media, from socializing, or from something else. Set a start time and a finish time. What are your feelings about such an experiment? Write down what you're feeling and then pray through what you've written with God.

8

LET US KEEP
THE FEAST

*Celebrating God's Goodness
in the Meals We Share*

Unless one learns how to relish the taste
of Sabbath while still in this world, unless
one is initiated in the appreciation of
eternal life, one will be unable to enjoy the
taste of eternity in the world to come.

ABRAHAM JOSHUA HESCHEL

The hour was not late, but dusky blues had started to descend much earlier than I had anticipated. Only two months into living in Scotland, I had not been aware how much the closer proximity to the arctic circle would affect the change of light during the day, and how rapidly the evening hours would converge on the final wisps of daylight as autumn gave way to winter's shadows. In the intensity of my study, the day had passed me by faster than I had expected, and the steely blue outside had suddenly deepened into a burnished sapphire. The hour was not late, but I was. And the darkening sky only served to further irritate my foul mood.

The burn of frustration was more than my tardiness; it was wrapped up into the fears waiting in the corners of my mind, the bourgeoning uncertainties that I had held back with such aplomb for weeks but which were now converging on me. Months earlier, I had made the decision to pack up my life in the United States and move myself four thousand miles across the Atlantic to a tiny fishing village on the Scottish coast, where I would do postgraduate studies in theology and the arts. My hopes had been set high, but the inflow of new information, like drinking out of a fire hose, had begun to overwhelm me. What had seemed certain to me before about life, artistry, and theology was being constantly overturned in the incessant influx of seismically upending new knowledge. I stared into the void of my own uncertainty as I prepared my first real attempt at getting at something, in essay form; did I really have anything worthwhile to say?

In my heart, I knew my apprehension wasn't even really about my new educational pursuit; it only served to heighten the real cause of my uncertainty. After years of constantly pursuing the road of opportunity and vocation, intermittently leaving the familiarity of a given place and resetting my world in a new, unfamiliar one, after years of starting from scratch with new community after new community, I had simply become weary. Once again I had made the leap into the unknown, this time beyond even the bounds of my own nationality into a world far beyond the borders of my known life. I was suspended in the limbo of the time between day and night, between knowing and unknowing. So much change and reorientation, so often the tumbling down to the foot of the mountain of familiarity, staring up at the distant peak of belonging, wondering if I would ever reach the top. I thought of my family, so far away, celebrating Thanksgiving without me, and I felt the jolt of fear run through me, the fear of being lost in the wilds on my own, without the safe shore of the known.

Mercifully, my dim thoughts were cut short as I trudged the few final steps through the dark to my friend's house, shrugging off the shadows pressing down on me. As I walked through the door, the world transformed.

"You made it! I'm so glad!" said my friend as I shook off the cold and hung up my coat. "Come in and have something to drink. We didn't want to start until you were here."

At the verge of the door, a savory aroma wafted around me, and suddenly the dark began to dissipate into the alluring fragrance, pulling me further in. Before I knew it, a full glass of cider was placed in my hand, conversation bubbled up with half a dozen friends gathered in the living room, and the heat of my former worries and frustration began to burn off like a mist. Soon our host, a fellow transplant from the States, clinked their glass to bring us to attention and place us at our set spots around the table. Together we gathered, prayed, and prepared ourselves, and for the first time in the evening, I recognized an unusual feeling in myself, a sense of anticipation, even without being able to put my finger on it.

In moments, steaming sweet potatoes, squash casserole, and several different kinds of dressings had materialized on the table, each casting its enchantment on me and piquing my appetite for what I knew was coming, the pièce de résistance of any good Thanksgiving meal: the turkey. Locating a full-sized turkey in Scotland is no small task, and my friend had gone above and beyond; each fillet was expertly carved, with a caramelized honey glaze, and baked to perfection. I knew then, with a sudden realization, how much work had gone into this sumptuous feast, and I was moved with gratitude for what the glorious spread before us testified. Soon, plates were filled with orange and green and gold, and the elements of each dish were distributed to everyone. Once again, I felt the spirit of hope rise within me, as if something I couldn't quite see, and yet was waiting just around the corner of the evening, was nearly upon me, something that would scatter my darkness and recall me to the light.

The first few bites surprised with a dazzling array of spices and herbs and seasoning. As the warmth and nourishment began to fill me, my heart began to feel at ease, and before I knew it, we were smiling and laughing and telling stories. Soon, we sent each dish around for seconds, and then for thirds, and then finally, it was time for dessert.

As we shared in rich, boutique coffee purchased by our host just for this evening and awaited the sweet completion to our veritable banquet, I thought of home, of family gathered together thousands of miles away. My heart yearned with desire to be with them; and yet somehow, to my surprise, the sadness and emptiness I had experienced before in thinking of them had been wiped away. I marveled at myself, until I looked around at the people gathered with me, and as I beheld the friendship and camaraderie in their eyes, I felt the love of my family being expressed through each of them. In our shared meal, I had somehow received the remembrance of the goodness that I had been missing, in participation with each of them.

Finally, the realization came to me: This is what my heart had anticipated. *This is what I was made for*: community, and communion, for the joy of the feast. Each bite had reinstated me to the remembrance of those who loved me and to the goodwill of those gathered there, expressed to me in their shared fellowship. Each savoring of a new flavor returned me to that truth and grounded me in the comfort of that knowing. In the joy of the feast, I drew the fading past of my family and friends and community into the present of those around the table with me, finding the heart of belonging once again through their kindness. The feast we shared became the sign of our mutual love, the joy of that communion.

This is because the feast is at the heart of the whole of God's story, and at the very middle of it is the invitation into communion.

The Nourishing Story

In the beginning, there was a garden; and at the end of all time, there will be a wedding feast; in the very center of history is also a meal, the food of bread and wine given in bodily form for the salvation of the whole world. In each chapter of the story of creation, the Fall, salvation, and restoration, God's love and kindness overflow in the plenitude of nourishment, given for us. In a way, feasting sums up the whole conviction of this book, the essence of every twist and turn of our journey through the senses: The life which we are called into in Christ is not one of mere observation, of contemplation and belief, but rather, a life of participation, of taking Jesus into ourselves and letting Him transform and transfigure us from the inside out. What is most important about our faith is not what we believe; God has not merely given the idea of Himself to us to contemplate, but instead His real and incarnated self, to be known and loved and sought after in relationship. What is most important about us is that in which we participate, that which we make part of ourselves.

The lifeblood of feasting in Christian life flows from the meal at the center of our worship, a meal itself summing up the thrust of salvation history from the beginning: from the tree of life in the Garden of Eden, given so that those created in His image might participate in His life; to the manna given to the Israelites in the wilderness, sustaining and strengthening them in their long wandering; to the life of Jesus Himself, expressed in the abundance of fish and loaves, the symbolic potency of bread and wine, and the radical self-sacrifice of body and blood. In every corner of Scripture, every twist and turn of God's story points to a singular truth: God is the founder of the feast, and the food which He lays before us is His own self, through Jesus. In participating in the Supper of the Lamb, we express, with all those who have come before us throughout the history of the church, that our very life force comes from the God who lives in and through us, who has given Himself as the nourishment which we, in thanksgiving, offer back to Him.

And not only does it reinstate us to our calling in this age; it reveals our future in the next. What are we destined for? Every time we participate in the Lord's Supper, we declare it through our actions: We are not merely destined to be restored to God's presence but rather to participate in His eternal life, through Him and in Him.

Many of the great formularies of Christianity express this sense of Communion. The Reformed Westminster Confession of Faith states that "Man's chief end is to glorify God, and to *enjoy* him forever."[1] The Orthodox Church in America states, "Man, according to the scriptures, is created 'in the likeness of God' (Gen. 1.26-27). To be like God, through the gift of God, is the essence of man's being and life."[2] The Roman Catholic catechism quotes Augustine, saying: "Man is made to live in communion with God in whom he finds happiness: When I am completely united to you, there will be no more sorrow or trials; entirely full of you, my life will be complete."[3] In each of these sweeping statements is a unique unity of thought: the very purpose for which we were created, the vocation set into the very fiber of our human nature, is to participate in His life. The purpose of our human lives is to partake of God, to make ourselves one with Him.

How ought we to think of this communion? How should we participate in God's feast? I want to take us on a journey, looking at the scope of our everyday meals, always with an eye aimed at the meal at the very center of Christian praise, the meal of the Communion table. In Communion, time converges on itself, and the feast draws both our *remembrance* and our *anticipation* into the posture of *receiving* the fullness of joy from our good God. Our feasts outside of worship are echoes of the feast at the heart of worship.

The earliest Christians expressed this in their first sacramental rites as a community. Before the Eucharist had become its own separate rite, it was first part of the *love feast*, the *agape* (a word indicating an exemplar form of love sourced in God), a joyful communal meal shared among the whole Christian community. The celebration of the Lord's Table, the rite at the very center of worship commanded by Jesus Himself, was seen as emerging from this spirit of the feast. And though the sacrament of Communion would soon become formalized, that spirit has ever been at the heart of Eucharistic theology. No experience of eating in community is ever really devoid of the in-breaking presence of the founder of all our feasts, the God of abundance who never gives a stone when His children ask for bread.[4] In each section of our consideration of feasting—to *remember*, to *anticipate*, and to *receive*—we will consider the spiritual life infused in eating in these ways and then connect that with the glory present in the meal of meals, the feast that sacramentally sums up all our feasts, the Communion table itself.

Before we start in with the feast itself, however, we begin with the invitation of fragrance. Among all the senses, aroma and taste have a uniquely interactive relationship; they work in tandem, from the moment of the first whiff of the prepared meal to the very heart of participation in it. Each enlivens the other, spurring the other on to the greatness present in the feast. The invitation to the feast, the sense which makes us aware of the meal and draws us out of our passivity into action, is aroma itself, like the messenger who carries good news to us.

Called by Aroma

The first clarion call of the feast is its aroma. Before we see the meal and its various delicacies, before we taste each flavor and savor each bite, we are met with a scent. Even if we are far away, the scent comes to us, seeks us out like a messenger.

The scent of the feast is what awakens us to its goodness and draws us out of our passivity into action. Aroma doesn't merely provide an alternative notion to whatever has occupied our attentions in a given moment; rather, it arrests our affections, rouses us out of our dreariness. When we receive the fragrance of the feast, something is brought to life within us. We no longer wish simply to remain where we are but feel that we must give some response to this call. The scent is the *invitation*, the call to *vocation*. Our idle hands and hearts are given purpose, to come and be put to work in the celebration at hand. Aroma calls us to come forth and feast.

Aroma is the priming of our longings; it prepares them by shocking our senses into life, drawing them into awareness and expectation. It is the first sign that the feast is not merely a utilitarian act of necessity but rather a participation in something alluring and desirable, something that responds to a longing planted within us.

Our scent capacity is also what gives us the knowledge of whether the meal to which we have been invited is fresh or whether there is something spoiled in it, something which might put us off or harm us. Scent helps us practice the discernment of good feasting from bad feasting, of that which will restore, delight, and replenish from that which will disgust or even bring distress. Many idioms in the English language give credence to the role of scent in the process of preliminary evaluation: When we want to express that someone has a natural, innate proclivity for a given pursuit, we say, *they have a nose for it*; when we want to express to someone the importance of trusting their instinct, we tell them to *follow their nose.* Even the most simple, self-explanatory phrase communicates it: *The nose knows.*

Just as all meals in some way reflect the glory of the Eucharistic feast (as we will soon discover), so does the role of aroma in our everyday lives reverberate with the same resonance of the way aroma prepares us for worship. Scripture itself alludes to the way in which our praise acts as the aromatic prelude to our communion with God. As we have already seen, in Psalm 141, the psalmist pleads with God that the praise offered might be received as a fragrant aroma:

"May my prayer be set before you like incense; may the lifting up of my hands be like the evening sacrifice."[5] In this instance, it is the psalmist who offers God praise. The aroma of the feast is the remembrance of God's goodness through Christ, made manifest again, its pleasant fragrance an enticing invitation to leave our seats and journey to the table, where His feast has been laid for us.

It is in this remembrance that scent works its most powerful enchantment. Perhaps the most foundational role of fragrance is in the way it awakens memory. Some psychological studies have shown that scent, among all the senses, is perhaps the one most associated with memory, most connected to recollection of past events. When we receive the scent of a good meal, we are suddenly transported; our memories of that same food, shared in the past with friends or family, are animated and brought to life, as if drawing the past into the present moment. Scent is the pathway which transcends the immutable wall of the past; like passing through a wormhole in time, the countless seconds, minutes, hours, and days are made as if nothing at all, as if the love crystallized in the memories of the past spills out suddenly into the current moment.

And in allowing that recollection to be restored anew through fragrance, we are also, even if unconsciously, lit with an inner fire of anticipation. When one becomes aware of the renewal of the feast in their own space and time, it plants within them an awareness that what was exclusively imprisoned in the past is liberated into the here and now. And at the same time, this moment itself may indeed someday be a past which is drawn into a future present. It is as if all the sequence of the many returns and departures to and from the table, in the past and in the future, are aligned with this moment, a moment that expresses the hope for what will one day be, yet already is becoming now.

In the invitation of aroma, which calls out to us in our quietness and stillness, we leave the time of our everyday life and enter into a sacred time, a time of the feast, when the past and the future draw close to the present moment of the meal before us. And yet the time of the feast is neither truly past nor present but instead catalyzes them both to change the experience of the present. Suddenly, the present, the still point of the "now" which so quickly evades our grasp, begins to inexplicably expand, so that what is contained in the fleeting moments of fellowship at the table contains a plenitude far exceeding the bounds of the possible.

Aroma initiates this entry into the time of the feast, and that time is brought into fullness of life through our subsequent journey to the table, where we consummate the invitation of aroma into participation in the feast itself.

Feasting to Remember

One of the oldest traditions in my family is our annual "shepherd's meal," celebrated on Christmas Eve. Like the shepherds in the fields might have enjoyed on the night of Christ's birth, we share in a simple spread of modest, hearty elements. We prepare an assortment of nuts, cheeses, and fruits, along with warm bread straight out of the oven and freshly made potato soup. As we bring all the bounty to the table and gather around it, we light the candles and enter into the simplicity of the story through a reading of Luke 2, the story of the shepherds who receive the message of Christ's birth from angels.

In our shepherd's meal, we eat to place ourselves in the midst of the story. Each year, the nourishment of the simple meal we have celebrated many times throughout our lives has become inextricably interwoven into the story of the shepherds themselves, accustomed to quietly attending their own pastoral rhythms, day after day. Like them, we allow our hearts to be inculcated into the modest goodness of a shared evening meal, and to let that posture prepare us to enter the astonishment and wonder at the miracle of the angelic visitation. From the familiar preparation, to the setting of the table, to warm fellowship and enjoyment of the feast, to the reading of Scripture, the shepherd's meal becomes our reenactment, our way of returning to the posture of humble participation that the meal has engendered in us in past years and which we make new over and over again. And when we partake of the food laid before us on the table, we make that story our own, invite it to become part of us, to nourish us from the inside out. It does more than remind us of the story; it makes it fresh and new to us again. In the feast, we are called to *remember*.

When we eat at the table, we are, in essence, returning: returning to be nourished and returning to fellowship. We return because we must; we admit that we are not capable of surviving on our own, that we are in need of the food which replenishes our energy and restores us to vitality. The table acts as the gathering place where we recall our need and admit that we must seek the resolution of that need outside ourselves. And equally, when we come together around the table, all who are gathered eat of the same food, declaring, even if tacitly, that this need is a universal one, and we are unified in our belonging to this table through that cycle of departure and return. The table recalls us to our belonging, the space in which we are made one through participating in one meal together.

Remembering is the first and most fundamental role of feasting in the Christian tradition, and it is written into the first statements Jesus makes about the meal of His own table. At the Last Supper, as Jesus prepares to enter the final moments of His life, He gives the meal to His disciples in the upper room as a memorial, a living sign which, though they don't understand it yet, after the crucifixion, will become an indelible, tangible point of return for them to participate in His love offered completely on the cross. Jesus knows that the disciples have come to this Passover table to remember God's faithfulness to His people, liberating them from Egyptian oppression and setting them on their journey to the Promised Land. Now, Jesus is transforming that act of remembrance so that forevermore, the disciples—and all who will become Jesus' disciples thereafter—will participate in that meal as an act of recollection of Jesus Himself. "He took some bread and gave thanks to God for it. Then he broke it in pieces and gave it to the disciples, saying, 'This is my body, which is given for you. Do this in remembrance of me.'"[6]

Just like the disciples so long ago, the sign of our faithfulness today is not to churn up new ideas, new feelings about God, but rather to return to the signs of His faithfulness given at the very beginning and to participate in them, to call the past into the present of our lives and make it manifest in the here and now. When we eat at the Lord's Table, when we take the elements of bread and wine into ourselves, in a sense, we allow that moment in the upper room to live again, to become real to us in our own time, through our bodies.

The Anglican Book of Common Prayer powerfully articulates this in a passage that comes from its morning prayer liturgy and is used in some churches in festival seasons as part of the Eucharistic liturgy: "Alleluia. Christ our Passover Lamb has been sacrificed for us;* therefore let us keep the feast."[7] The spirit of this Eucharistic feast isn't only contained within the conventional bounds of Communion on a Sunday but rather flows out into each and every day.

For what is given at the Table of the Lord is not a one-time action that achieves its given end in perpetuity. Our souls, like our bodies, must return to the Table, for we are prone to forget, prone to grow lean and frail the longer we are away from the one in whom we have life abundant. Our hunger for restoration, for healing, for nourishment, drives us back to the Table of the Lord, the space where we are tangibly recalled to the grace that sustains us. When we eat at the Communion table, we return to the source of our being, remembering that it is only through Jesus' presence *in us* that we have been restored to new life; as we eat the bread and drink from the goblet, the tastefulness of that brief meal enters us and recalls us to that inner presence.

Over time, this invitation to remembrance instills within us not only a recollection of the past in the here and now but an equal looking toward the future reconciliation of all life in Christ, when we will all feast at the Table of the Lamb.

Feasting to Anticipate

In his delightful book *The Supper of the Lamb: A Culinary Reflection*, Robert Farrar Capon, an Episcopal priest and an aspirational chef, shared his love for cooking by interspersing recipes and hospitality advice with his own theological reflections on the spirituality of eating. Just when the reader thinks Capon is explaining the secrets for getting a particular dish just right, suddenly they find they are being ushered through the use of water in cooking as a vibrant analogy for heavenly purity, or the way in which the host acts as a priest of their household, mediating grace through their hospitality. The book is filled with both uproarious humor and surprising poignancy, often paired with each other back-to-back.

The last chapter of the book captures this rather well, in which Capon rather hilariously touches on the delicate subject of heartburn, a possible unfortunate occurrence even in the best of feasts. After a lengthy elocution on the merits of potential remedies, Capon suddenly shifts to what he calls "the higher distress for which earth has no cure—that major, vaster burning by which the heart looks out astonished at the world and, in its loving, wakes and breaks at once."[8] This, he says, is a kind of internal fire for which there is no cure in this world, a fire which can only be quenched by something beyond it; an "inconsolable heartburn." This is, as Capon suggests, the very purpose of the desire to eat: "We were given appetites, not to consume the world and forget it, but to taste its goodness and hunger to make it great."[9]

We eat because we must, yes, and the return to the table for our nourishment can never be extracted from our participation in a meal. And yet, the heart of the feast is about more than survival; it is far more wrapped up in delight, in the vibrant goodness of delectable tastes and flavors which heighten our senses and make us more aware of the goodness present in our lives. When we relish in a well-cooked meal, we allow ourselves to be interwoven into the ever-bourgeoning life of creation itself through partaking of its produce, the very source of the meal in which we participate. We allow creation's glory to become our glory, and we allow its longing for completion to be made manifest in us as well. The great paradox of the feast is that as quickly as the pleasure of an excellent meal has kindled our taste buds, it begins to fade. The brilliance and delight of taste, in which is contained an immeasurable expression of pleasure and transcendence, is known only in the most fleeting of moments that arouse within us the desire for the return to it even as soon as it has passed. In this way, the joy of a meal is in what it leaves unanswered, ungratified. To feast is to put our desire into action, to heighten it. The feast enlivens within us a hunger for a completion of the joy of what we receive only in part now. It gives us a taste of the coming feast, when we will "never again be hungry or thirsty,"[10] as Revelation tells us.

The anticipation present in our everyday feasting is present in Christ's table too. In some forms of Catholic liturgy, when the priest presents the raised elements of the Eucharist to the gathered congregation, he intones the words: "Behold the Lamb of God, behold him who takes away the sins of the world. Blessed are those called to the supper of the Lamb."[11] While it is clear from the liturgy that the text is speaking to the here and now of the moment when the congregation will participate in the meal of the Communion table, the source of the text provides a surprising additional resonance to the words. It comes from Revelation, where John speaks of the completion of time, when the people of God will join in the wedding feast of Christ in heaven: "The angel said to me, 'Write this: Blessed are those who are invited to the wedding feast of the Lamb.'"[12] By using this verse as the basis for the participation in the Lord's Supper, such liturgy imbues Communion with an *eschatological* sensibility, a sensibility which anticipates the end of time, and the putting to rights of all things. It articulates that our participation in Communion is not only a remembrance but an expectation; an anticipation for the time when our joy in the feast is no longer fleeting but is made complete.

And our participation in this feast, both our remembrance

of what draws us back to the table and our anticipation of what it foreshadows, is predicated entirely on one thing and one thing alone: that we are guests by virtue of God's abundance, not through our capacity to bring anything to the table but rather through our willingness to receive with open hands.

Feasting to Receive

In his poem "Love," the seventeenth-century devotional poet George Herbert imagines himself as a poor and ill-prepared guest who has traveled far and has finally arrived at the house of Love. As the last poem of Herbert's collection *The Temple*, a poetic examination of the Christian everyman's journey through life with God, the poem stands out all the more as the expression of the ingrained feeling of unworthiness; how even after a lifetime's work pursuing God, his soul remains "guilty of dust and sin." As he stands on the precipice of the final doorway into the house where God has prepared His celebratory feast, Love's disposition is all the more arresting in the face of how little the Christian has to offer, and how profound Love's kindness is nonetheless:

> Love bade me welcome: yet my soul drew back,
>> Guiltie of dust and sinne.
> But quick-ey'd Love, observing me grow slack
>> From my first entrance in,
> Drew nearer to me, sweetly questioning,
>> If I lack'd any thing.[13]

Notice how in the movement described in the poem, it is constantly the speaker who withers away from Love's kindness and how even in spite of that withdrawal, Love still "drew nearer to me." Love ever moves to draw the broken and imperfect unto itself. The second stanza makes this contrast of movement even more manifest:

> A guest, I answer'd, worthy to be here:
>> Love said, you shall be he.
> I the unkinde, ungrateful? Ah my deare,
>> I cannot look on thee.
> Love took my hand, and smiling did reply,
>> Who made the eyes but I?[14]

In this second exchange, the speaker once again renews his objection to his worthiness to be present. To this, Love heightens and develops its pursuit of the speaker, not only by drawing close but by coming into contact, by taking the hand of the unworthy guest. Finally, the speaker begins to relent, but not before one final inquiry of Love:

> Truth Lord, but I have marr'd them: let my shame
>> Go where it doth deserve.
> And know you not, sayes Love, who bore the blame?
>> My deare, then I will serve.
> You must sit down, says Love, and taste my meat:
>> So I did sit and eat.[15]

Love finally reveals the truth of its pursuit: It intends to give itself as the feast which justifies the speaker's presence in the house of Love. Love, who has approached the unworthy soul, then laid on that soul its own hands of grace, now offers it the food of transformation, that what Love has expressed is made manifest. As the unworthy soul eats, the food of Love becomes wrapped up into its own being, transforming it and making it new again.

Herbert encapsulates how in the end, the beauty of the feast is not in our preparedness for it but in the fact that God has laid a table for sinners, for misfits, for the worthy and the unworthy alike. All are welcome, not because they have earned the feast but because God has made them worthy through His overflowing, abundant love, a love which knows no scarcity or limit. At the very heart of the table is the feast of love God has prepared for us, the meal of Himself which He has given in full, holding back nothing. As Herbert so elegantly expresses, the trepidation we experience in approaching the Table of the Lord is in ourselves; it is we who object to our own presence at the feast. We forget that "It is He who has made us, and not we ourselves";[16] where we see imperfection, God sees the beauty of His handiwork.

The poem reminds us that it is not through our efforts, our impoverished sense of value, that we are worthy of approaching the table. We can do nothing to prove to God that we have somehow met the standards of perfection required in approaching Him. The sacrament of the Lord given at His table, like all sacraments, and like the whole of the sacramental world He has created and through which He seeks us, is given as pure gift, flowing from the infinite love and grace of His very self. Many traditions include a corporate confession prior to participation in the table; while it may seem like confession operates as a work that earns us the right to call ourselves worthy, it is quite the opposite; in confession, we radically let go of the sins that we hold so tightly, willingly leaving them at the foot of the cross. The cross is the threshold of the home for which our hearts are made, and when we go over that threshold, we confess that we have emptied ourselves and are ready to receive the gift of Christ. This means we must give up and abstain from the foods that spoil our appetites for Jesus alone, that make us feel either that we are not worthy or that, conversely, make us believe we have merited our place at the table. Confession helps us to turn away from both the indulgent food of our own self-righteousness and the harmful fare of our self-despair. To confess is not only to admit something wrong; it is also to declare something right. To confess is to proclaim that we have emptied ourselves of everything, our sins and our merits, and are hungry only for God. To be ready to participate in a meal means beginning with an empty stomach, primed through hunger to be filled. This is the only way to receive the feast, to accept this radical posture of reception, emptying ourselves of all that so easily entangles us, so that we might receive the fullness of Jesus.

Many Christian traditions, including Methodists, Presbyterians, Anglicans, and Catholics, make use of a pre-Communion prayer entitled the Prayer of Humble Access, which gives language to this stance of reception:

> We do not presume
> to come to this your table, merciful Lord,
> trusting in our own righteousness,
> but in your manifold and great mercies.
> We are not worthy
> so much as to gather up the crumbs under your table.
> But you are the same Lord
> whose nature is always to have mercy.
> Grant us therefore, gracious Lord,
> so to eat the flesh of your dear Son Jesus Christ
> and to drink his blood,
> that our sinful bodies may be made clean by his body
> and our souls washed through his most precious blood,
> and that we may evermore dwell in him, and he in us.
> Amen.[17]

The words of the Prayer of Humble Access help to place us, as the participant in the Communion table, in a willing stance of reception, like a helpless baby bird, openmouthed and utterly dependent on the food which is given entirely by the merit of the one who brings the meal to them. We trust and rely on the everlasting mercy of God, and we make this surrender our conviction in the assurance of that mercy. And through that relinquishing of ourselves, we are brought into mysterious new life of Christ *in* us, which Paul so marvelously tells us is "the hope of glory."[18] It is this indwelling which sums up the feast—and truly, the whole of our encounter of Jesus through our senses.

The Great Invitation

At the end of his life, the great medieval theologian Thomas Aquinas, who had written some of the most profoundly masterful works of theological expression in the history of the church, was given a vision of Jesus in His heavenly glory. After the vision, Thomas put down his pen and never picked it up again. He died soon after, leaving his magnum opus, the *Summa Theologiae*, unfinished. When his assistant exasperatedly asked why he would not continue writing, Thomas simply replied, "All that I have written seems to me nothing but straw—compared with what I have seen and what has been revealed to me."[19]

Perhaps one could see Thomas's action as one of despair, realizing the insufficiency of even the greatest of human achievements to come close to the limitlessness of God's profound glory. But what if it was exactly the opposite? What if, rather than despair, Thomas had received such an intense infusion of the grace of Christ's beautiful presence that the lesser efforts of his earthly life were giving way to participation in the eternal joy of Christ's love for him? In communion with Christ, all else falls away, and only the gift of eternal life and abundance remains.

This is the spirit of the feast: that in Jesus, we are given an invitation into participation. No longer need we wait at a distance, trying to understand, grasping at some sense of assurance or knowledge. In Jesus, we are offered true food and true drink, sustenance that restores us, body and soul. Spread before us is a meal that nourishes our most manifest needs, piques our appetite for the good, the true, and the beautiful, and enlivens our desire for full communion. And this meal is freely given to all who are willing to receive it openhandedly as a gift.

This spirit of the feast is the summation of the whole of this book: God has given Himself in a sumptuous banquet through Christ, allowing His limitless life to overflow into our world and reach out to us in every encounter of our senses. At the heart of this overflowing grace is the expression of gift, that all is given freely to us. God withholds nothing from us, and all we need do is receive. Every rhythm expressed in this book, every activity or posture or disposition, is laid out before us, gathered in a sumptuous and abundant meal, inviting us to come and dine. Each sense is an ingredient in the lavish meal of the divine life set before us, and together, all those elements make up the whole of the masterful meal to which we are invited.

From the Communion table, where we encounter the mystery of Jesus and participate in Him, to the table of the whole universe, in which Jesus offers us the bounty of His presence in all things and through every encounter with our senses, the whole world is a great invitation into God's infinite life. The question that remains is simple: Will you dine at the table of the Lord? Will you participate?

COMMON SENSES

- What aromas do you associate with your childhood? How clearly can you recall them? What memories are connected to those aromas?

- What does your faith "smell" like? Is it the cologne or perfume of the people you sit near during worship? Is it incense or some other scent that is used in a worship service? A meal you share with your small group? How do you find these aromas shaping the practice of your faith?

- When was the last time you feasted in the name of the Lord? Who was there? What was on the menu? What else did you do besides eat? When can you do it again?

EPILOGUE

Dancing the Drama into Life

The tired wood flooring creaked and groaned under the weight of the many feet gathered in the bustling, mingling crowd. Friends and strangers shared smiles and laughter, stuffed too close together and bumping unceremoniously into each other as the throng grew energetic. Just as I was certain the room had reached its full capacity of people and noise, a voice soared over the clamor.

"Ladies and gentlemen, it's the time you've all been waiting for! Please clear the floor, link arms with the person to your left and the one to your right, and make a big circle!"

A burst of laughter bubbled up as the mass of people began shifting. Soon enough, strangers became friends and linked arms with any available moving body, until the floor in the middle opened into a wide sea of unclaimed space.

The ceilidh had begun.

I had only just arrived in Scotland to study theology at the ancient University of St Andrews a few weeks prior. But I knew from the gathering buzz in conversations with new friends that I wouldn't go long without finding myself at a ceilidh, a traditional Scottish community gathering full of lively music, vibrant storytelling, and most important of all, *dancing*. My expectations were high, and I'd been excited to join in the fun. But now, in the midst of it all, I felt self-consciousness rising up in me. Everything was new and unfamiliar, and while everyone else seemed to know what to do, I found myself feeling squarely on the outside.

The crowd surged together, but I drew back toward the safety of the wall, where I could observe the festivities from a distance. I scanned the room for a familiar face to save me from the awkwardness of my vigil on the edges of the dance floor; eventually, my gaze found a friendly face. My friend locked eyes with me and smiled widely, gesturing enthusiastically for me to join. I shook my head and smiled back. I tried to look at ease, just another face enjoying the evening; but in my mind, I heard: *I can't join in. I don't know the steps to the dance.*

From somewhere vaguely in the same direction as the previously heard announcer, an accordion burst out into a merry jig, and the voice boomed energetically over the melody.

"Ladies and gentlemen, the Circassian Circle!"

Suddenly, feet began to move in time together, lilting toward the center, and then out wide once more. First up were the ladies; three spirited steps in, a rousing clap, and then back out again. Now it was the men's turn; they jaunted forward and whooped as they clapped their hands, and then they, too, returned to their place in the great circle and faced their partners. First a playful mosey back and forth, and then dozens of couples twirled round and round in each other's arms, spinning like tops on a table. And then, just as quickly, everyone was in a circle again, moving a few steps forward to begin again.

I looked at my watch absently; only a minute had passed by. I sighed and tried to settle my mind and enjoy the frivolities. I decided to wait it out a couple more dances and then amble over to the bar and see if I might catch some conversation.

From beside me, a woman's bright Scottish brogue broke into my thoughts.

"You're not just going to sit here all night like a neap head and miss all the dancing, are you?"

I turned to take in my new friend. A pair of sparkling eyes caught me in their stare and dared me to respond. She raised her eyebrows mischievously, and the edges of her mouth turned up ever so slightly.

I shrugged sheepishly and smiled. "It's okay, just watching. I'm afraid I don't know the steps!"

And then, in a sudden flurry, without even a hint of a reply, the stranger drew me forward into the fray. There was no going back now; I had been cast into the dance.

At first, I waited, unsure of what to do; my new partner sailed forward into the circle and clapped, and then she stood by my side again.

"Your turn!" She said with a grin and an encouraging nudge.

Before I knew it, I moved forward, carried by the momentum of the music and the sway of the motion. Three strides in toward the center of the circle, with a clap and whoop, then out again. Now my new companion and I faced each other. First, we moseyed side to side in a flowing sway, our toes lightly leaping back and forth; the lilt of it made me grin, and I felt the uncertainty melting away. But my newfound confidence froze, as I thought, *What comes next?*

"Don't worry," she said reassuringly. "Just take my arms and turn me! Here, like this!"

With a strong grip, she took my right forearm with hers, and crossed her left arm over to my left arm, and we began to spin. Round and round we circled, whirling breathlessly, color and harmony and laughter all blending together. For a moment, time ceased, and the movement was all stillness; in the turning of the steps of the dance, my heart, before so restless and uncertain, relaxed. Our feet turned and dipped and spun, as shuttles threading through a loom, miraculously never meeting, but circling in and around each other simply. As readily as I'd learned the steps, the motion took over, and I fell into it gleefully. The face of my new friend shined, a joyful spirit in both our eyes.

Then, just as suddenly as it had started, the music sounded

its final cadence, and we slowed to a stop. Everyone bowed to their partners, laughing heartily, and my new friend and I exchanged a proper introduction. The normalcy of the evening returned.

In my heart, I was no longer a mere observer waiting on the outside; the spirit of the dance had taken me and woven me into its patterns.

I am now much further into my life here in Scotland, and whenever I'm able, I relish the chance to walk into the boisterous experience of a ceilidh. Each traditional tune speaks to me like an old familiar friend; from the gentility of "Gay Gordons" to the spirited step of "The Dashing White Sergeant" to the joy of the crowd favorite, "Strip the Willow." The harmony and melody may enter through my ears, but they come back out through my feet. The ancient rhythms of these dances have become as familiar as rain, and when I hear the band strike up, that first joyous experience comes back to me. I can't help but leap into the fray, returning to that feeling of transcendence waiting just past the edges of the music.

Go Forth and Dance

Friends, after a long and spirited jig, our song is drawing to an end, and everyone is beginning to applaud. Like my friend did for me on that spirited Scottish evening, I have taken you by the hand and brought you into the dance. I have taught you some of the steps and shown you how to make your way from one side of the dance floor to the other. This song is over; but the band is tuning their instruments, and another tune is surely soon to strike up again. What will you do? You can simply fade into the crowd again, draw back from the light and the spiritedness and the exuberance, stay in the safety and anonymity of the shuffling crowd on the margins. Or you can leap into the fray again, take a risk, and let yourself learn the steps anew.

There's nothing more I can teach you that you can't learn on the dance floor of the whole world itself. The life of the Spirit is in that dance, in the willingness to participate and come into contact with the given, tangible world around you. I hope you can see by now that the life of the senses isn't something to be explained or understood. It is something to be *experienced*, a clarion call to *participation*. Yes, there is risk; you might miss a step or two or find yourself twirling left when everyone else is twirling right. You will inevitably stumble from time to time. But caught in the midst of the dance, you will be lifted up again by the hand of Jesus, who is the master of the dance, the one for whom it came into being and the one who leads it onward. The world is spinning in a glorious caper, moving through sight and sound and taste and touch and smell. In each of these expressions, Jesus reaches out to you, through your experience, inviting you to step in time with Him, and to know the jubilation of His glorious movement in the world. For the whole world is His, and He loves all that He has made.

May all your steps be blessed, friends, may the dance come

to be a familiar and beloved rhythm in accompaniment with the Holy Spirit; and in your every movement in the world, may you encounter the Lord who loves you and will never stop reaching out to you in everything, even your senses.

NOTES

INTRODUCTION

1. *Hungry*: Kathryn Scott, "Hungry (Falling on My Knees)," *Hungry (Falling on My Knees)* © 1999 Vineyard Music; *Desperate*: Hillsong Worship, "Touch of Heaven," *There Is More* © 2018 Capitol Christian Music Group; *Open*: Paul Baloche, "Open the Eyes of My Heart," *Open the Eyes of My Heart* © 2000 Integrity Music.
2. Lulu Garcia-Navarro, "'Dirt Is Good': Why Kids Need Exposure to Germs," NPR, July 16, 2017, https://www.npr.org/sections/health-shots/2017/07/16/537075018/dirt-is-good-why-kids-need-exposure-to-germs.
3. Alister E. McGrath, *Christian Theology: An Introduction*, 5th ed. (Malden, MA: Wiley-Blackwell, 2011), 188.

1: LET BEAUTY AWAKEN

1. John 1:1-4.
2. Colossians 1:15-17.
3. Colossians 1:20.
4. J. R. R. Tolkien, *The Silmarillion*, ed. Christopher Tolkien (London: HarperCollins, 1998), 17.
5. Leonard Cohen, "Anthem," *The Future* © 1992 Columbia.
6. The following story is a creative adaptation of Mark 8:31-33, 9:2-8.
7. Colossians 1:27, niv.
8. Psalm 19:1.
9. Psalm 19:4.

2: TO RISE WITH THE MORNING STAR

1. Hebrews 1:3.
2. Hans Boersma, *Heavenly Participation: The Weaving of a Sacramental Tapestry* (Grand Rapids, MI: Eerdmans, 2011), 24. Emphasis added.

3. Proverbs 4:23, NASB.

4. Matthew 15:11, 19-20.

5. Proverbs 27:19, NIV.

6. C. S. Lewis, "Bluspels and Flalansferes: A Semantic Nightmare," *Selected Literary Essays*, ed. Walter Hooper (Cambridge: Cambridge University Press, 2013), 265.

7. Psalm 37:4, NIV.

8. Proverbs 3:5-6, NIV.

9. St. Augustine, *Confessions*, trans. Benignus O'Rourke (London: Darton, Longman and Todd, 2017), 3.

10. "Selected Liturgical Hymns," Orthodox Church in America, accessed March 11, 2020, https://www.oca.org/orthodoxy/prayers/selected -liturgical-hymns.

11. Alexander Schmemann, *For the Life of the World: Sacraments and Orthodoxy* (Yonkers: St Vladimir's Seminary Press, 1997), 102.

12. S. D. Smith, *The Green Ember* (Beckley: Story Warren Books, 2014), 220.

13. The Episcopal Church, *The Book of Common Prayer*, 2016 revised edition, accessed March 11, 2020, https://episcopalchurch.org/files/bcp_04-28 -2017.compressed_0.pdf.

14. Robert Taft, *Liturgy of the Hours in East and West: The Origins of the Divine Office and Its Meaning for Today* (Collegeville, MN: The Liturgical Press, 1986), 350–51.

15. C. S. Lewis, *Surprised by Joy* (London: William Collins, 2016), 209.

16. Madeleine L'Engle, *Walking on Water: Reflections on Faith and Art* (Colorado Springs: WaterBrook, 1998), 17.

17. L'Engle, *Walking*, 17.

18. L'Engle, *Walking*, 56.

3: CHARGED WITH THE GRANDEUR

1. Ephesians 2:10, NIV.

2. Alfred Lord Tennyson, *In Memoriam A. H. H.*, canto 56, st. 1.

3. Tennyson, *In Memoriam*, canto 56, st. 4.

4. Tennyson, *In Memoriam*, canto 56, st. 5.

5. Tennyson, *In Memoriam*, canto 56, st. 7.

6. G. M. Hopkins, "God's Grandeur," found in *Poems of Gerard Manley Hopkins*, ed. Robert Bridges (London: Humphrey Milford, 1930), 26.

7. Hopkins, "God's Grandeur," 26.

8. *The Tree of Life*, directed by Terrence Malick (Los Angeles: Fox Searchlight Pictures, 2011), DVD.

9. *The Tree of Life*, directed by Terrence Malick (Los Angeles: Fox Searchlight Pictures, 2011), DVD.

10. *The Tree of Life*, directed by Terrence Malick (Los Angeles: Fox Searchlight Pictures, 2011), DVD.

11. Saint Francis, "The Canticle of Brother Sun," in *Francis and Clare: The Complete Works*, trans. Regis J. Armstrong and Ignatius C. Brady (New York: Paulist Press, 1982), 38.

12. Saint Francis, "Canticle of Brother Sun," 39.

13. Saint Francis, "Canticle of Brother Sun," 39.

14. Colossians 1:20, NIV.

15. Romans 8:22.

16. Romans 8:23.

17. Genesis 32:26.

18. Ephesians 2:10.

19. J. R. R. Tolkien, *On Fairy Stories*, eds. Verlyn Flieger and Douglas A. Anderson (London: HarperCollins, 2008), 77.

4: CREATION'S SONG

1. Quoted in "Proms 2014: Commemorating the Outbreak of WWI with John Tavener and the Tallis Scholars," *The New Statesman*, August 5, 2014, https://www.newstatesman.com/culture/2014/08/proms-2014 -commemorating-outbreak-wwi-john-tavener-and-tallis-scholars.

2. William Blake, "The Lamb," found in *The Complete Poetry and Prose of William Blake*, ed. David V. Erdman (Berkeley : University of California Press, 2008), 8.

3. Blake, "The Lamb," 8.

4. Blake, "The Lamb," 8.

5. Gregory of Nyssa, *Treatise on the Inscriptions of the Psalms*, trans. Ronald E. Heine, in Ronald E. Heine, *Gregory of Nyssa's Treatise on the Inscriptions of the Psalms: Introduction, Translation, and Notes* (Oxford: Oxford University Press, 2001), 90.

6. Gregory of Nyssa, *Treatise*, 91.

7. Hans Boersma, *Embodiment and Virtue in Gregory of Nyssa: An Anagogical Approach* (Oxford: Oxford University Press, 2013), 70.

8. The Episcopal Church, *The Book of Common Prayer*, 2016 revised edition, accessed March 11, 2020, https://episcopalchurch.org/files/bcp_04-28 -2017.compressed_0.pdf , 112.

9. John O'Donohue, *Beauty: The Invisible Embrace* (New York, Perennial, 2004), 62.

10. Ecclesiastes 3:11.

11. O'Donohue, *Beauty*, 62.

12. Hebrews 1:3.

13. 1 Peter 1:3-4.

14. 1 Peter 1:8.
15. Olivier Messiaen, "Préface," as quoted in Richard D E Burton, *Olivier Messiaen: Texts, Contexts, and Intertexts (1937–1948)*, ed. Roger Nichols (New York: Oxford University Press, 2016), 44.
16. Rebecca Rischin, *For the End of Time: The Story of the Messiaen Quartet* (Ithaca, NY: Cornell University Press, 2006), 69.
17. James MacMillan, "God, Theology and Music," *New Blackfriars* 81, no. 947 (January 2000): 17.
18. Psalm 34:18, NIV.
19. Isaiah 53:3.
20. "The 'O Antiphons' of Advent," United States Conference of Catholic Bishops, accessed March 11, 2020, http://www.usccb.org/prayer-and -worship/prayers-and-devotions/prayers/the-o-antiphons-of-advent.cfm.
21. Jonathan Arnold, *Sacred Music in Secular Society* (London: Routledge, 2016), 38.
22. John 1:5.
23. 2 Corinthians 4:7, NASB.
24. Ryan O'Neal, "Saturn," found on Sleeping at Last, *Atlas: Space II* (Wheaton: Astroid B-612, 2013), mp3 recording.
25. 2 Corinthians 12:9.
26. 2 Corinthians 12:9-10.

5: DIVINE LIGHT THROUGH EARTHLY GLASS

1. "Second Council of Nicaea—787," in *Decrees of the Ecumenical Councils*, ed. Norman P. Tanner, trans. Joseph Munitiz, William Rearsall, Edward Varnold, et al. (London: Sheed & Ward, and Washington, DC: Georgetown University Press, 1990), 135.
2. Colossians 1:15.
3. Tanner, "Second Council," 136.
4. Eugène Burnand, *The Disciples Peter and John Running to the Sepulchre on the Morning of the Resurrection*, 1898, oil on canvas, 83 × 135.5 cm, Musée d'Orsay, Paris, https://www.musee-orsay.fr/en/collections/index -of-works/resultat-collection.html?no_cache=1&zoom=1&tx_damzoom _pi1%5Bzoom%5D=0&tx_damzoom_pi1%5BxmlId%5D=009239&tx _damzoom_pi1%5Bback%5D=en%2Fcollections%2Findex-of -works%2Fresultat-collection.html%3Fno_cache%3D1%26zsz%3D9.
5. Philippians 2:15-16, NIV.

6: TO TOUCH THE FACE OF GOD

1. Rene A. Spitz, "Hospitalism: An Inquiry into the Genesis of Psychiatric Conditions in Early Childhood," *Psychoanalytic Study of the Child* 1, no. 1 (1945):53–74.

2. Isaiah 61:1.

3. Wendell Berry, *Sex, Economy, Freedom and Community: Eight Essays* (New York: Pantheon Books, 1993), 122.

4. "Ubi Caritas," *Thesaurus Precum Latinarum*, accessed July 13, 2020, http://www.preces-latinae.org/thesaurus/Hymni/UbiCaritas.html.

5. John 13:34, NIV.

6. "Ubi Caritas," *Thesaurus Precum Latinarum*, accessed July 13, 2020, http://www.preces-latinae.org/thesaurus/Hymni/UbiCaritas.html.

7. Mark 9:35.

8. Matthew 19:30.

9. John 15:13.

10. Henri J. M. Nouwen, *Life of the Beloved: Spiritual Living in a Secular World* (New York: Crossroad, 2002), 59.

11. Nouwen, *Life of the Beloved*, 63–64.

12. Nouwen, *Life of the Beloved*, 112.

13. Michelangelo Merisi da Caravaggio, *The Incredulity of Saint Thomas*, 1603, oil on canvas, 107 × 146 cm, Sanssouci Picture Gallery, Potsdam, https://www.caravaggio.org/the-incredulity-of-saint-thomas.jsp.

14. Mother Teresa, *A Simple Path*, comp. Lucinda Vardey (New York: Ballantine, 1995), 79.

15. As quoted in Dave McAuley, *Summit Life Today: 101 Inspirational Leadership Lessons* (Bloomington, IN: WestBow Press, 2015), chap. "Helping the Poor."

16. 1 Corinthians 11:24.

7: THE HOLY ART OF WINDOW WASHING

1. Peter C. Bouteneff, *Arvo Pärt: Out of Silence* (Yonkers, NY: St Vladimir's Seminary Press, 2015), 143.

2. John 1:4, NIV.

3. Luke 1:78-79.

4. Psalm 30:5.

5. Matthew 27:65-66.

6. "J. S. Bach St Matthew Passion: Text, Translation and Musical Notes," trans. Robert Minett and Anja Haerchen, Aberdeen Bach Choir, accessed March 12, 2020, http://www.aberdeenbachchoir.com/April2012/April2012DetailedMusicNotes21.html.

7. "J. S. Bach St Matthew Passion: Text, Translation and Musical Notes," trans. Robert Minett and Anja Haerchen, Aberdeen Bach Choir, accessed March 12, 2020, http://www.aberdeenbachchoir.com/April2012/April2012DetailedMusicNotes21.html.

8. Joseph Ratzinger and William Congdon, *The Sabbath of History* (Washington, DC: William G. Congdon Foundation, 2000), 38.

9. Ratzinger and Congdon, *Sabbath of History*, 40.

10. Ratzinger and Congdon, *Sabbath of History*, 42.

11. Bonaventure, *The Journey of the Mind into God*, trans. Oleg Bychkov, 49, http://web.sbu.edu/theology/bychkov/itinerarium_oleg.pdf.

12. Bonaventure, *The Journey of the Mind into God*, trans. Oleg Bychkov, 50, http://web.sbu.edu/theology/bychkov/itinerarium_oleg.pdf. Emphasis in original.

13. Wolfgang Sandner, *Program Notes for Arvo Pärt's Tabula Rasa*, trans. Anne Cattaneo, ECM New Series 1275, 1984, compact disc, as quoted in Marguerite Bostonia, "Bells as Inspiration for Tintinnabulation," in *The Cambridge Companion to Arvo Pärt* (Cambridge: Cambridge University Press, 2014), 128.

14. Bouteneff, *Arvo Pärt*, 36.

15. Bouteneff, *Arvo Pärt*, 40.

16. Bouteneff, *Arvo Pärt*, 42.

17. Psalm 30:5.

8: LET US KEEP THE FEAST

1. Presbyterian Church in America, *Westminster Confession of Faith and Catechisms* (Lawrenceville, GA: Christian Education and Publications Committee of the Presbyterian Church in America, 2007), 355, https://www.pcaac.org/wp-content/uploads/2019/11/ShorterCatechismwith ScriptureProofs.pdf. Emphasis added.

2. "Man," Orthodox Church in America, accessed March 10, 2020, https://www.oca.org/orthodoxy/the-orthodox-faith/ spirituality/orthodox-spirituality/man1.

3. Catechism of the Catholic Church, "Section One: 'I Believe'—'We Believe,'" The Holy See, accessed March 10, 2020, https://www.vatican.va /archive/ccc_css/archive/catechism/p1s1c1.htm.

4. Matthew 7:9.

5. Psalm 141:2, NIV.

6. Luke 22:19.

7. Anglican Church in North America, *The Book of Common Prayer and Administration of the Sacraments with Other Rites and Ceremonies of the Church* (Huntington Beach, CA: Anglican Liturgy Press, 2019), 16, http:// bcp2019.anglicanchurch.net/wp-content/uploads/2019/08/BCP2019.pdf. The asterisk denotes a break in the antiphonal call and response.

8. Robert Farrar Capon, *The Supper of the Lamb: A Culinary Reflection* (New York: Random House, 2002), 188.

9. Capon, *Supper of the Lamb*, 189.

10. Revelation 7:16.

11. ICEL, "The Order of Mass," from the *English Translation of The Roman Missal* (London: Catholic Bishops' Conference of England and Wales, 2011), https://www.liturgyoffice.org.uk/Missal/Text/MCFL.pdf.

12. Revelation 19:9.

13. George Herbert, "Love," in *The English Poems of George Herbert*, ed. Helen Wilcox (Cambridge: Cambridge University Press, 2007), 661.

14. Herbert, "Love," 661.

15. Herbert, "Love," 661.

16. Psalm 100:3, NASB.

17. "Holy Communion Service," The Church of England, accessed March 10, 2020, https://www.churchofengland.org/prayer-and-worship/worship -texts-and-resources/common-worship/holy-communion.

18. Colossians 1:27, NIV.

19. As quoted in Josef Pieper, *Guide to Thomas Aquinas* (San Francisco: Ignatius Press, 1991), 158.

THE NAVIGATORS® STORY

T HANK YOU for picking up this NavPress book! I hope it has
  been a blessing to you.

NavPress is a ministry of The Navigators. The Navigators began
in the 1930s, when a young California lumberyard worker named
Dawson Trotman was impacted by basic discipleship principles and
felt called to teach those principles to others. He saw this mission as
an echo of 2 Timothy 2:2: "And the things you have heard me say in
the presence of many witnesses entrust to reliable people who will
also be qualified to teach others" (NIV).

In 1933, Trotman and his friends began discipling members of the
US Navy. By the end of World War II, thousands of men on ships and
bases around the world were learning the principles of spiritual multi-
plication by the intentional, person-to-person teaching of God's Word.

After World War II, The Navigators expanded its relational ministry
to include college campuses; local churches; the Glen Eyrie Conference
Center and Eagle Lake Camps in Colorado Springs, Colorado; and neighbor-
hood and citywide initiatives across the country and around the world.

Today, with more than 2,600 US staff members—and local ministries in more than 100 countries—The Navigators continues the transformational process of making disciples who make more disciples, advancing the Kingdom of God in a world that desperately needs the hope and salvation of Jesus Christ and the encouragement to grow deeper in relationship with Him.

NavPress was created in 1975 to advance the calling of The Navigators by bringing biblically rooted and culturally relevant products to people who want to know and love Christ more deeply. In January 2014, NavPress entered an alliance with Tyndale House Publishers to strengthen and better position our rich content for the future. Through *THE MESSAGE* Bible and other resources, NavPress seeks to bring positive spiritual movement to people's lives.

If you're interested in learning more or becoming involved with The Navigators, go to www.navigators.org. For more discipleship content from The Navigators and NavPress authors, visit www.thedisciplemaker.org. May God bless you in your walk with Him!

Sincerely,

DON PAPE
VP/PUBLISHER, NavPress

www.navpress.com

CP1308